Crafts All Year Round

First published by Parragon in 2009

Parragon
Queen Street House
4 Queen Street
Bath BA1 1HE, UK

ISBN 978-1-4075-3807-5

Printed in China

SESAME STREET

Crafts

All

year

Round

PaRragon

Bath · New York · Singapore · Hong Kong · Cologne · Delhi · Melbourne

CONTENTS

This book is full of creative, fun things to make for your family, your friends, and yourself for all kinds of occasions.

GETTING STARTED

SPRING CRAFTS

SUMMER CRAFTS

FALL CRAFTS

WINTER CRAFTS

LET IT RAIN CRAFTS

ANYTIME CRAFTS

TIPS FOR PARENTS AND CAREGIVERS

This book is for the whole family. Its primary purpose is to bring together parents and children, from preschoolers to teens, to have fun making things! True, making things with young children can take time and get a little messy. But it will be fun and it will give them a sense of achievement. Once children start making things, they just might become "crafters" for life.

The Importance of Doing Crafts with Children

The projects that appear in this book were designed for, worked on, and tested by young children and their families. Every craft project in this book highlights at least one task that a young child can perform. Make sure to choose projects with steps that you think your own child can accomplish with relative ease. Remember, what seems like a small, simple task to you—applying glue to the back of a piece of paper, coloring in a simple design, or arranging shells in a dish—is a big accomplishment for a small child, and can instill a sense of pride.

From the time a child picks up his first crayon until he reaches adulthood, he goes through several developmental stages with regard to arts and crafts—from scribbles (about age 2); to assigning meaning to shapes drawn (about age 5); to the creation of three-dimensional objects (about age 8.) Although the pace at which each child progresses may differ, important skills can be developed by working with crafts.

LEARNING SKILLS
- Logic, problem solving
- Basic math skills (measuring; using a ruler; using measuring cups)
- Reading (looking at directions or reading a recipe)
- Following sequential directions
- Creativity and artistic sensibility
- Self-esteem and a sense of uniqueness
- Fine and gross motor skills
- Eye-hand coordination
- Cleaning skills (including responsibility)
- Fun!

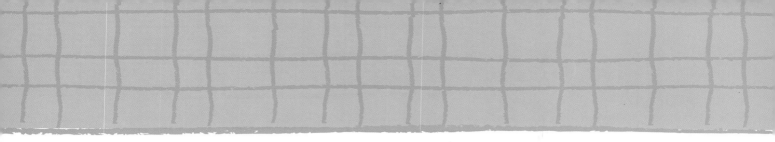

How to Use This Book

The crafts included here all require the supervision (and usually the hands-on help) of an adult, especially with preschool-aged children. However, each craft contains at least one "kids!" icon (featuring a *Sesame Street* character) indicating a step that your preschooler should be able to accomplish, depending on the skills and abilities of your individual child. Also included with each craft are special features written for the children that bring "words of wisdom" (or just fun thoughts!) from the *Sesame Street* friends.

The first step in creating each craft is to read through the directions for the project from beginning to end. That way you and your child will know what materials and tools you will need. If she is able, encourage her to read familiar numbers out loud from the materials list, and pick out her favorite letters of the alphabet. Although understanding written fractions can be difficult for preschoolers, you can certainly point out "½" in a materials list and explain the concept of "one half" by showing her that if you cut one whole pipe cleaner into two equal parts, you now have two halves.

Finally, although directions for these crafts are often quite specific in order to ensure clarity, remember that part of the fun of making crafts is to be creative. We encourage you to experiment with color, found objects, or decorating in any way that seems appropriate and appealing. Don't worry if the end result doesn't look exactly like the photo. Half the fun of crafting is developing your own style and expression.

A Few Thoughts on Safety

Avoid accidental choking. It's natural for very young children to put small objects, such as beads, magnets, and crayons, into their mouths. Please supervise your child, no matter what age, at all times. Make it very clear that none of these materials belong in the mouth, then keep a watchful eye.

Keep away from hot or sharp objects. When making your crafts in the kitchen, be sure you are working at a safe distance from a hot stove and sharp objects, such as knives.

Tie back long hair; roll up sleeves. Both you and your child should wear an apron, or old clothes, since they might get spattered with glue or paint.

Clean up before and after working with crafts. Start with a clean work surface so your materials will stay clean. After you've finished, clean up thoroughly.

Work slowly and carefully. Just do one step at a time.

GET CRAFTY

It's a good idea to keep all your craft materials together. You can design a special craft box, or purchase an inexpensive plastic container from an office supply or container store. Create a special craft workspace (if you have the space) and cover it with a plastic or paper tablecloth, newspaper, or other protection as you work.

Essential Tools

Here's a useful list of essential tools and materials you'll need to do most of the projects in this book.

- Scissors (those with rounded tips are safest for younger children)
- A set of acrylic paints in basic primary colors (red, blue, yellow, black and white)
- Paintbrushes in various sizes and thicknesses
- White glue and an old paintbrush to apply it
- Colored pencils; colored markers; crayons
- Black fine-tipped marker
- Pencils
- Ruler
- Large eraser

More useful materials

Here are some other materials you might want to have on hand. Look out for things to collect or interesting materials to store at home until you are ready to craft. This is a great way to reuse things and make less trash in the world.

Gift wrap

Recycled gift wrap can come in handy for many projects. If it's too crumpled, iron it with a cool iron, and it will be as good as new.

Cardboard

Use recycled cardboard from packing boxes, cereal boxes, laundry detergent boxes, or other cardboard packages to make your projects.

Fabric

Worn out blue jeans can be turned into bags, purses, and pencil cases. Scraps of patterned fabric can be used to make bean bags, pouches, as a coverings for boxes, or as decorations in infinite ways.

Odds and ends

Save odd buttons, earrings, and other old jewelry in cookie tins, then use them as craft decorations. Even old bottle caps (both metal and plastic) can be used in creative ways.

Objects from nature

When you are outdoors in the park or garden, pick up pretty leaves, interesting twigs, feathers, pinecones, seed heads, stones, and other objects from nature. At the beach, collect shells, pebbles, and driftwood.

TIPS FOR SUCCESS

Prepare your space

Cover your workspace with newspaper or a plastic or paper tablecloth. Make sure you and your children are wearing clothes (including shoes!) that you don't mind becoming spattered with food, paint, or glue. But relax! You'll never completely avoid mess; in fact, it's part of the fun!

Wash your hands

Wash your hands (and your child's hands) before starting a new project, and clean up as you go along. Clean hands make for clean crafts! Remember to wash your hands afterward, too, using soap and warm water to get off any of the remaining materials.

Follow steps carefully

Follow each step carefully, and in the sequence in which it appears. We've tested all the projects; we know they work, and we want them to work for you, too. Also, ask your children, if they are old enough, to read along with you as you work through the steps. For a younger child, you can direct her to look at the pictures on the page to try to guess what the next step is.

Measure precisely

If a project gives you measurements, use your ruler, T-square, measuring cups, or measuring spoons to make sure you measure as accurately as you can. Sometimes the success of the project may depend on it. Also, this is a great opportunity to teach measuring techniques to your child.

Be patient

You may need to wait while something bakes or leave paint, glue, or clay to dry, sometimes for a few hours or even overnight. Encourage your child to be patient as well; explain to her why she must wait, and, if possible, find ways to entertain her as you are waiting. For example you can show her how long you have to wait by pointing out the time on a clock.

Clean up

When you've finished your project, clean up any mess. Store all the materials together so that they are ready for the next time you want to craft. Ask your child to help.

SPRING CRAFTS

BIRD BATH

YOU WILL NEED

- Colored oven-bake clay
- Rolling pin and knife
- Metal or plastic plate with wide flat rim
- Plastic gloves
- Spatula
- Grout
- Old cloth
- Varnish
- Paintbrush

1

Roll out the clay thinly. Cut out enough square tiles to cover the plate rim. Harden the tiles in the oven following the manufacturer's instructions.

2

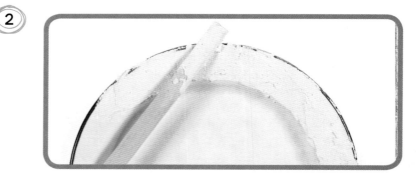

Put on the plastic gloves and use the spatula to spread a layer of tile grout across the rim of the plate.

3

KIDS

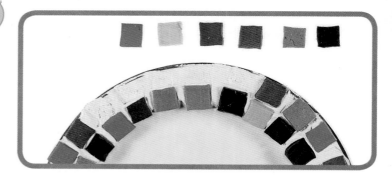

Press the tiles into the grout, working round the rim of the plate. Leave a narrow space between each tile. Leave to set for 24 hours.

④

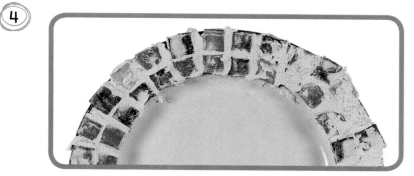

Use the spatula to carefully fill in between the tiles with more grout. Allow to dry for 24 hours.

⑤

Wipe off all of the extra grout, then polish up the tiles with a cloth. Now apply a layer of varnish with a paintbrush to give them a shine.

DID YOU KNOW?
All birds have wings but not all birds can fly!

Try using craft jewels to decorate your plate.

BIRD FEEDER

YOU WILL NEED

- Empty milk or juice carton
- Scissors
- Paint and paintbrush
- Strong tape
- String
- Birdseed

1

Cut away the four sides of the milk or juice carton, leaving space at the base to hold the birdseed.

2

KIDS

Paint your bird feeder inside and out. You may want to choose a color that will blend in with the surroundings, such as green or brown.

3

Decorate your bird feeder. Then attach a piece of strong tape in a loop to the top of the feeder and fill the base with some birdseed.

4 Hang up your bird feeder with string in a place safely out of the reach of cats.

DID YOU KNOW? It's hard for birds to find food in winter. You can help by making bird feeders and keeping them filled.

Thread some peanuts on string and hang it up by the feeder. Birds will love it!

PLATE GARDENS

YOU WILL NEED

- Old dinner plate
- Potting compost
- Pebbles
- Twigs and yarn
- Dried moss and flowers
- Selection of leaves
- Scissors
- Paper
- Sand

1 KIDS

Spread a layer of potting compost on a plate, leaving the rim uncovered. Use tiny pebbles to make a path, and make bean poles from twigs tied with yarn. Use some moss to make a hedge.

2 KIDS

Plant your garden with leaves and flowers. You could make some clay models of vegetables or tools for your garden.

3

To make this spring scene, use twigs and yarn to make a clothes line. Cut a picket fence from paper, and some laundry from paper.

Plant up the garden, using moss for the bushes, and press dried flowers into the earth to make a pretty flower bed.

DID YOU KNOW? Flowers are very important! Many birds and insects eat their nectar, pollen, and seeds.

Make a snowy winter scene. Use modelling clay for a snowman and sprinkle salt for snow.

19

BOTTLE GARDENS

YOU WILL NEED

- Sticks
- Old spoon
- Wire
- Kitchen sponge
- Cottonball
- Large jar with lid
- Pebbles or gravel
- Suitable potting compost
- Suitable plants, such as ivy and vine
- Paint
- Awl or screwdriver

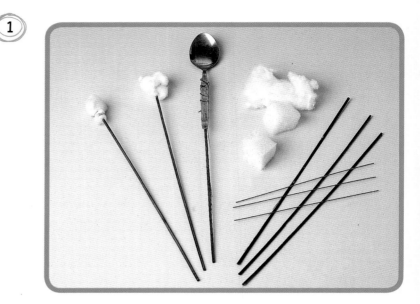

Use an old spoon attached with wire to a long stick for a digging tool. Use sponge wired onto a stick to press the earth down when planting. For a cleaning tool, use a cottonball wired onto a stick.

2

KIDS

Pour a thin layer of pebbles or gravel in the base of the bottle. Now cover the pebbles with a thick layer of potting compost. Press the compost down with your sponge tool.

③

Use the digging tool to place individual plants in position. Press the compost down firmly around the plants. Use the cottonball tool to clean up the sides of the bottle garden.

④

Carefully make holes in the lid using the awl or screwdriver. Use paint to decorate the bottle garden with any pattern you like. Put the lid on and place your garden in a place with lots of daylight, but not in direct sunlight.

DID YOU KNOW?
Plant roots grow lots of tiny hairs near their tip to "drink" in water from the soil.

Choose low-growing plants, and water your bottle garden every two weeks in the summer.

PLANT POTS

YOU WILL NEED

- Old gardening pots, margarine or yogurt tubs, kitchen containers
- Acrylic paint in different colors
- Paintbrushes

1 KIDS

Make sure the pots are clean and dry. Paint on a base coat, then cover the pot completely. You may need to do several coats of paint to cover it well. Let dry.

2 KIDS

Paint any pattern you like on the pot. It's fun to paint on things such as borders, flowers, or animals. Practice drawing some ideas on paper before painting them on the pot.

To make smaller plant pots, paint your yogurt cartons in lots of bright colors. They make perfect containers for smaller, or young plants or herbs.

DID YOU KNOW? Green plants use energy from light to grow and stay a healthy green color.

To keep from making a mess, Elmo covers the work area with newspapers before beginning.

DESERT GARDENS

YOU WILL NEED

- Flowerpot
- Gravel
- Old spoon or small garden trowel
- Cactus potting compost
- Cactus plants
- Suitable gloves
- Selection of stones
- White sand

1 KIDS

Place a layer of gravel in the flowerpot. This will provide drainage for your plants.

2 KIDS

Add a layer of cactus potting compost and press it down firmly.

Put on your gloves, then dig small holes in the compost and plant the cacti.

Me like painting lizards, snakes, and desert animals on pots.

Cover the compost with a layer of white sand. This will make it look like desert sand. Add stones to make it look like a desert scene. Place your pot by a window and water the plants when the soil gets dry.

MINI BUG POTS

YOU WILL NEED

- Air-drying clay
- Water
- Acrylic paints
- Paintbrushes
- White glue and brush
- Water-based varnish

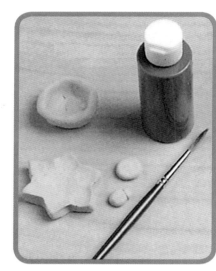

1 Push your thumbs into a ball of clay to make the pot shape, smoothing it with your fingers. Make a lid out of a flat disk of clay. Stretch it into a flower shape, then make a ladybug from a ball of clay.

2
KIDS

Paint the pot, lid and ladybug, allowing them to dry between colors. When completely dry, glue the bug to the lid. Apply a coat of varnish over the whole thing.

3 KIDS

Experiment with different shaped pots and creepy crawlies. Let your imagination go!

DID YOU KNOW?
There are more kinds of insects in the world than any other type of creature.

Oh, what a cute little bug!

DRIED FLOWERS

YOU WILL NEED

- Florist's foam
- Knife
- Ceramic pot
- A selection of dried flowers
- White glue and brush
- Scissors
- Ribbon
- Acrylic paints

KIDS

1

Cut the florist's foam with the knife and fit it into the flowerpot. Ask a grown-up to help you do this.

Press bunches of dried flowers into the foam, around the edge of the flower pot. Try to keep them all at the same height.

Glue dried moss around the edge of the pot. Using scissors, trim the moss all the way around, so it is even.

4

Use a little glue to stick some dried flowers in the center to finish off your design. Trim off any untidy bits with a pair of scissors.

DID YOU KNOW?
Plants make oil in their leaves to stop them drying out in strong sunshine.

Tie ribbon around your pot or paint it with colorful patterns to make it look extra special.

PRESSED FLOWERS

YOU WILL NEED

- Fresh flowers
- Flower press or heavy book (e.g. dictionary)
- Scissors
- White glue and brush
- Items to decorate, such as ready-made cards or boxes

1 KIDS

Press the flowers flat in a flower press or inside a heavy book. Keep the flowers in place for about three weeks before you use them. Dried flowers crumble easily so handle them carefully.

2 KIDS

Use them to make greeting cards. You can buy prepared cards to decorate or make your own from good quality paper. Use a little glue to attach the pressed flowers to the card. Paint on a little varnish to give the picture a glossy finish.

Make a flower picture. Press a whole flower in your flower press, or book. When ready, stick it on the card. Choose a small frame and place the pressed flower in it.

④

If you press lots of flowers you may have enough to cover a small box. Varnish it.

DID YOU KNOW?
Bees like blue or violet blue flowers best. Most birds like red flowers best of all.

Make sure that your flowers have no insects in them. And especially, make sure you have permission to pick the flowers.

CRUNCHY SALADS

YOU WILL NEED

- Jar
- Saucer
- Marker pen
- Piece of cheesecloth
- Scissors
- Elastic rubber band
- Spoon
- Mung beans or other seeds for sprouting

1
KIDS

Choose a pretty-shaped jar, then wash and dry it thoroughly. Draw around the saucer on the cheesecloth. Make sure the circle is a few inches bigger all round than the top of the jar.

2

Cut out the circle with scissors. This will be the lid for the jar. You will need an elastic rubber band to hold the fabric in place on top of the jar.

3

Place a large spoonful of mung beans (or other seeds) in the jar. Cover with water and leave to soak for two hours. Strain away the water.

4

Put the lid on the jar. Wash the spouts with water three times a day and watch them grow. When they are long enough to eat (before the leaves appear) wash them thoroughly. Use them in salads for a crunchy, fresh taste!

DID YOU KNOW? Sprouted seeds are very healthy. They are packed full of vitamins.

Try sprouting alfalfa or sunflower seeds – but don't use garden seeds, which may have been sprayed with chemicals.

SUNSHINE PLATE

YOU WILL NEED

- Old dinner plate with a wide rim
- Plastic wrap
- Newspaper squares
- White glue and brush
- Paintbrush
- Scissors
- Gold paint

1
KIDS

Cover the plate with plastic wrap, then use white glue to stick layers of newspaper squares all over it. Make sure the plate is completely covered.

2
KIDS

Leave the plate in a warm, airy place to dry. Then apply another layer of newspaper squares. You will need to do at least six layers to make the plate strong enough.

3

When the newspaper is completely dry, lift it off the plate and carefully peel away the plastic wrap. Cut a zigzag pattern around the edge of the plate.

4 KIDS

Cover the plate with gold paint, and leave it to dry. Remember to paint both sides. You may need to do several coats to get a truly golden, sunshine finish.

DID YOU KNOW?
The sun is actually a star, just like those we see twinkling in the sky at night.

Decorate the edge of your plate with craft jewels to make it look like treasure!

MINI FARM

YOU WILL NEED

- Oven-bake clay
- Modeling tool
- Baking sheet
- Shoe box
- Colored paper
- Scissors

1 KIDS

To make a sheep, soften the clay in your hands. Roll a thin sausage of black. Cut four legs using the modeling tool. Shape the body and head out of a ball of white clay. Add a ball of black clay to make the face. Use the modeling tool to join the parts.

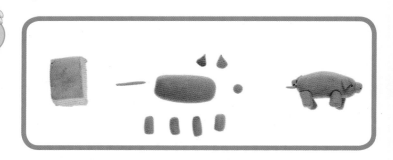

2 KIDS

Make a pig from pink clay. Cut four legs out of a sausage shape. Shape the body and head out of a ball of pink clay. Add ears and a snout.

3 KIDS

Make a hen from a squished ball of brown clay. Add a yellow beak and a red comb. Perch the hen on a flat disk of green clay.

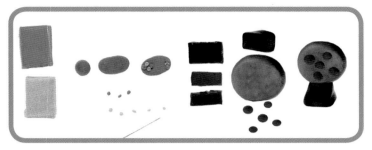

Make flower patches from green and yellow. To make a tree, use a sausage of brown stuck to a flattened ball of green clay.

5

Read the manufacturer's directions for the clay. Then place your models on a baking sheet, setting the correct time and temperature. While you wait for them to harden, decorate a shoe box with colored paper to keep your animals in.

DID YOU KNOW?
Pigs roll around in the mud to cool off!

What other animals can you make?

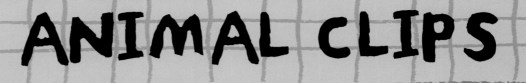

ANIMAL CLIPS

YOU WILL NEED

- Thin cardboard
- Pencil
- Scissors
- Marker pens: red, yellow
- Eraser
- White glue and brush
- Clothespins

1

KIDS

Carefully draw the outline of an animal's head on the cardboard with a pencil.

2

KIDS

When you are happy with your animal design, color it in using colored markers.

38

Then draw a dark outline around the colored animal. Cut out your animal and glue it onto a clothespin. Now it is ready to hold your notes!

DID YOU KNOW?
An adult lion's roar can be heard up to five miles away. ROARRR!

If you want, glue the clip onto a magnet and put it on the fridge.

3 KIDS

DOGHOUSE AND PET

YOU WILL NEED

- Empty milk or juice carton
- Scissors
- Paint
- Paintbrush
- Oven-bake clay or plasticene
- Modeling tool
- Marker pen

2 KIDS

①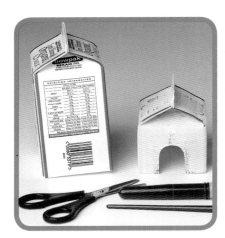

Cut the top off a clean empty carton. This will be the doghouse roof. Now cut a door in the front of the house for your pet.

②

Paint the house. It may need two coats. When it is dry you can write your pet's name above the doorway with a marker pen, if you want to.

③

Make a pet out of modeling clay. Use the modeling tool to join the parts together. Bake it in the oven according to the manufacturer's instructions.

When it is completely cool, you can put your pet in his new home. To help him settle in, why not make him a food bowl and snacks out of bits of leftover clay?

EASTER NESTS

YOU WILL NEED

- Shredded breakfast cereal
- 1 large and 1 small bowl
- Melted chocolate
- Spoon
- Foil or muffin cups
- Muffin pan
- White mint candies or yogurt-covered raisins

1

Line a muffin pan with foil or use muffin cups.

2 KIDS

Crumble the cereal into the large bowl. Check that there are no large chunks. Ask a grown-up to melt the chocolate in the small bowl.

3 KIDS

Stir the chocolate into the crumbled cereal and mix well with the spoon.

DID YOU KNOW? Easter eggs are a symbol of new life and springtime.

Place a spoonful of the mixture into each space and press it down into a nest shape. Leave the shapes to harden in a cool, dry place. Put them on a plate and add a few white mint candies to each one.

Decorate your plate with colorful paper streamers and daffodils to make it look really spring-like.

MOM'S PHOTO WALLET

YOU WILL NEED

- Thick cardboard
- Scissors
- Paper
- Glue
- Ribbon
- Pretty pictures from magazines
- Photographs

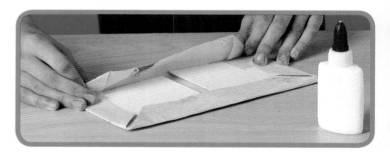

① You will need two equal-sized pieces of thick cardboard for the cover. Glue them onto colored paper, as shown, leaving a gap between them.

② Fold in the colored paper neatly and firmly, then glue it down, so that the outer edges of the two pieces of cardboard are completely covered.

③ Take a long piece of colored paper and fold it back and forth as if you are making a fan. This will make the pages of the wallet.

44

Glue a piece of ribbon to the inside of both cardboard covers, down the middle, and leave to dry. This will tie in a bow to keep your wallet closed.

5

Glue one end of the folded page section to the inside front cover. It should cover the ribbon, too. Glue the other end to the inside back cover.

Decorate the front cover with ribbon and a picture of something pretty cut from a magazine.

DID YOU KNOW? Mother's Day is celebrated in many countries around the world.

Fill the wallet with photos of you and all your family.

MATZAH COVER

YOU WILL NEED

- Rectangle of felt 10 x 12 inches
- Scraps of colored felt
- Ribbon long enough to fit around the felt rectangle
- Glue
- Pencil or marker pen
- Scissors
- Sequins

Glue four pieces of ribbon around the edge of the felt rectangle. Tuck the ends underneath, and glue in place.

2

Draw out the letters to spell "MATZAH" onto pieces of colored felt. Cut out the letters. Fold the felt 'A's in half for an easy way to cut out the holes.

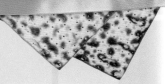

Glue the letters onto the felt background. Decorate with felt shapes and sequins.

Your Matzah cover is now ready to use.

DID YOU KNOW? Matzah has just two ingredients— flour and water!

SUMMER CRAFTS

BEACH SHOES

YOU WILL NEED

- Canvas shoes or flip flops
- Pencil and paper
- Fabric paints

1
KIDS

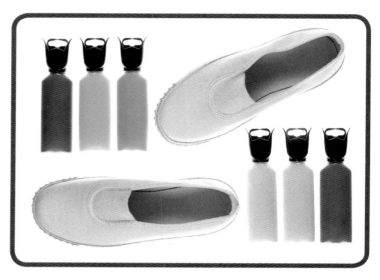

Sketch out a few ideas first on a piece of paper, then use fabric paints to draw fun shapes and doodles on your beach shoes or flip flops.

2
KIDS

Now color in your designs. Don't forget to wait for the paint to dry between different colors, and before you wear your shoes on the beach!

DID YOU KNOW?
Sand is shell and rock that has been worn down by nature into tiny grains.

LITTLE BOATS

YOU WILL NEED

- Selection of driftwood
- Paint (optional)
- Paintbrush
- Scissors
- Tissue paper
- White glue
- Thin twig

1 KIDS

Choose a piece of driftwood the right size and shape for the hull of your boat. You can paint it or leave it natural.

②

Use the scissors to cut out two triangles of colored tissue paper for the boat's sails. They can be the same, or different colors.

③

Use a thin twig for the mast. Glue it to the back of the hull and leave to dry. Then attach the sails by gluing one edge of each triangle to the mast as shown.

Can you think of any other things that float on water?

SEASHELL MOBILES

YOU WILL NEED

- Seashells
- String
- Scissors
- Paintbrush
- Varnish
- Driftwood or branch

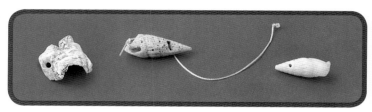

1

Thread the string through the first shell and tie a large knot underneath, to hold the shell in place. Find shells that already have holes in them, so you won't have to make them.

2

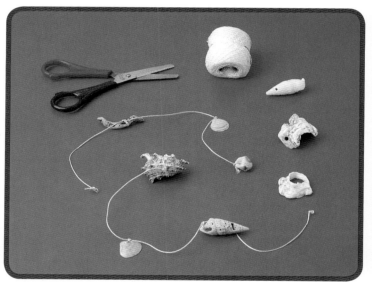

Continue threading on shells, tying a knot each time. Make as many separate shell strings as you like.

3

KIDS

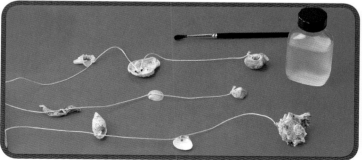

Varnish the shells and leave to dry.

④

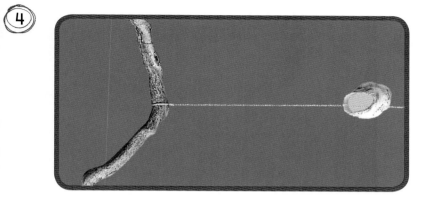

Make loops at the end of the shell strings to hang them from a piece of driftwood or a branch. Check the mobile for balance as you put them on.

⑤

KIDS

Hang up your pretty seashell mobile where you can see it, to remind you of a happy vacation.

FLOWER POTS

YOU WILL NEED

- Spatula
- Grout
- Ceramic plant pot or container
- Seashells
- White glue and brush
- Varnish
- Acrylic paints (optional)
- Paintbrush

1 KIDS

Use a spatula to apply a thick layer of grout along the rim of the pot.

2 KIDS

Press the seashells firmly into the grout. Leave the grout to dry.

3 KIDS

When dry, varnish the shells to bring out their natural colors.

4 KIDS

For a different look, paint your pot.

5 KIDS

When the paint is dry, use strong glue to attach some shells.

6 KIDS

When dry, varnish the shells. Leave to dry again, then put a plant in your pot.

PHOTO ALBUM

YOU WILL NEED

- Thin colored posterboard
- Scissors
- Hole punch
- Colored yarn or string
- Colored paper

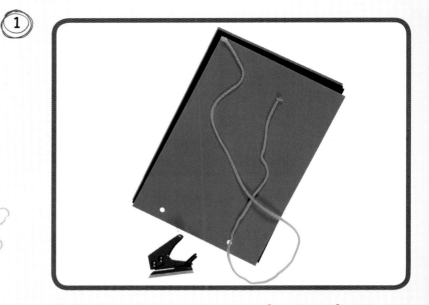

1

Cut two card rectangles for the front and back cover, and some paper pages for inside. Make two holes in the cover and pages, making sure they all line up.

2
KIDS

Thread some colored yarn or string through the holes and tie a knot or bow to hold the album together.

Cut a thin strip of paper. Fold it as shown to create a triangular "photo corner," cutting off the long extra bits of paper. Do this four times for each corner of your photo. Glue the back of each "corner" to stick the photo on a page.

Decorate the pages with colorful borders. Write the date, place, and who is in the photo, so you'll never forget.

Decorate the cover of your album with a picture or pattern. Then fill it up with your favorite photos.

SEASIDE JEWELRY

YOU WILL NEED

- Seashells and pebbles
- Jewelry clasps
- Earring hooks
- Varnish
- Paintbrush
- Wire
- Thread
- Scissors

①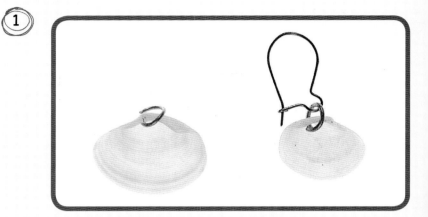

Some shells have tiny holes in them, but you can also use ready-made clasps from a craft shop to hold the shell in place. Attach an earring hook to each shell and you have a pretty pair of earrings.

2 KIDS

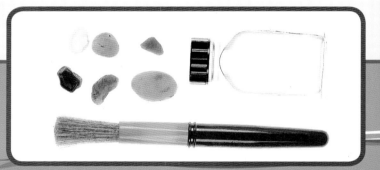

Find pebbles with interesting markings on them. Paint over them with clear varnish and leave to dry.

③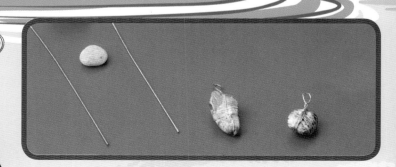

Wind a piece of wire around a pebble and make a loop at the top.

(4)

Attach a piece of thread to the loop and use this to hang your jewelry around your neck or wrist.

DID YOU KNOW?
If you hold a seashell to your ear, you can hear what sounds like waves on a seashore.

LIGHTHOUSE

YOU WILL NEED

- Shoe box lid
- Round plastic container (e.g. yogurt pot)
- Strong glue and adhesive tape
- Large stones
- Small pebbles
- Plaster of Paris
- Bowl and spatula
- Air-drying clay
- Acrylic paints
- Paintbrushes

1

KIDS

Glue the round container at one end of the cardboard lid. Position large stones around its base.

2

Mix up the plaster of Paris in the bowl. Pour it over the container and base of the lid.

3

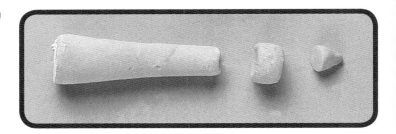

Use some air-drying clay to make a long cylinder, wider at one end than the other. Make the two smaller top sections separately. Leave the pieces to dry.

4

KIDS

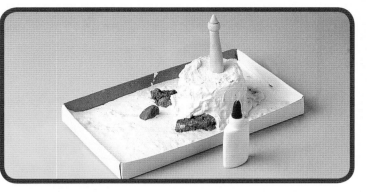

Glue everything in place and leave the model to dry.

5

KIDS

Spread glue over the hill and place pebbles over and around it.

What's your favorite thing to do on the beach?

6

KIDS

Once your model is dry, have fun painting and decorating your rocky, seaside scene.

PAPERWEIGHTS

YOU WILL NEED

- Pebbles
- Acrylic paints
- Paintbrushes
- Varnish

1 KIDS

Collect some interesting pebbles at the beach. Wash and dry them before you begin the craft.

2 KIDS

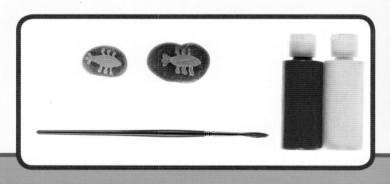

Use a fine paintbrush to paint on a pattern or picture.

3 KIDS

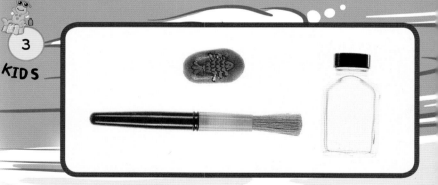

When the paint is dry, add a layer of varnish to protect the surface and give your paperweight a glossy finish. Let dry thoroughly before you use it.

DID YOU KNOW? Pebbles are smooth because they tumble and bang together in the sea, wearing the edges down.

TIC-TAC-TOE

YOU WILL NEED

- Thick colored cardboard
- 8 thin strips of wood or craft sticks
- Scissors
- Paintbrush
- Glue
- Shells
- Oven-bake clay

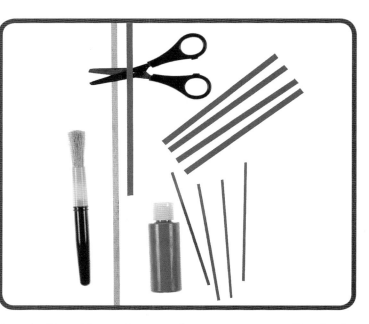

Paint the thin strips of wood or craft sticks in your chosen color. Leave them to dry.

2

Cut the cardboard into a square for your game board. It can be any size you like. Cut the thin strips of wood to length for the sides of your game board.

③

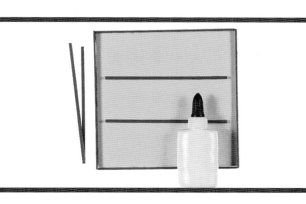

Glue the sides to the board. For the board markings, glue two more thin strips of wood on the board as shown.

④

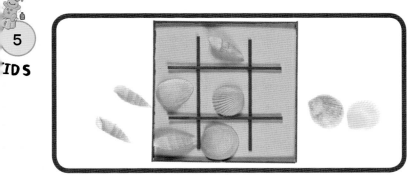

Glue the last two wood strips onto the game board top to bottom.

⑤

IDS

Make two sets of four counters out of pebbles, matching shells, or oven-bake clay. Make sure they fit in the spaces.

DID YOU KNOW?
This game is also known as "noughts and crosses" or "hugs and kisses."

Once you each have a counter on the board, try to stop the other player from getting three in a row. The first player to get a row wins!

SHELL FRAMES

YOU WILL NEED

- Thin cardboard
- Scissors
- Grout
- Spatula
- Selection of shells
- Varnish
- Paintbrush
- Adhesive tape

1

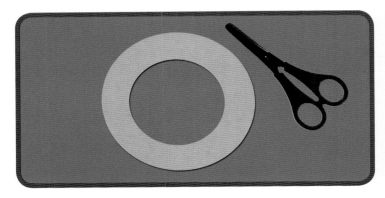

To make the frame, cut out a small circle from a piece of thin cardboard. Cut out a smaller hole out of the center. This will be the hole for your picture.

2 KIDS

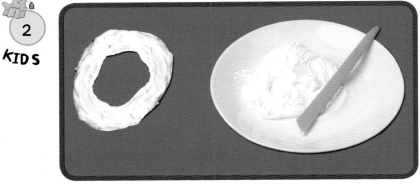

Apply a layer of grout around the frame using the spatula.

3 KIDS

Gently press in the shells in a fun pattern around the edge of the frame.

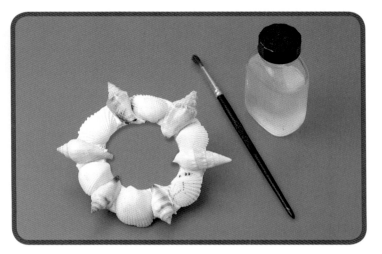

When the grout has dried, paint the shells with a layer of varnish.

5

Tape a photograph to the back of the frame with tape, so that the picture shows through the hole. Hang up the frame or use it as a small paperweight.

DID YOU KNOW?
Long ago, some people used shells as money!

Put one of your favorite beach photos in the frame, so the shells remind you of sunny days.

FATHER'S DAY

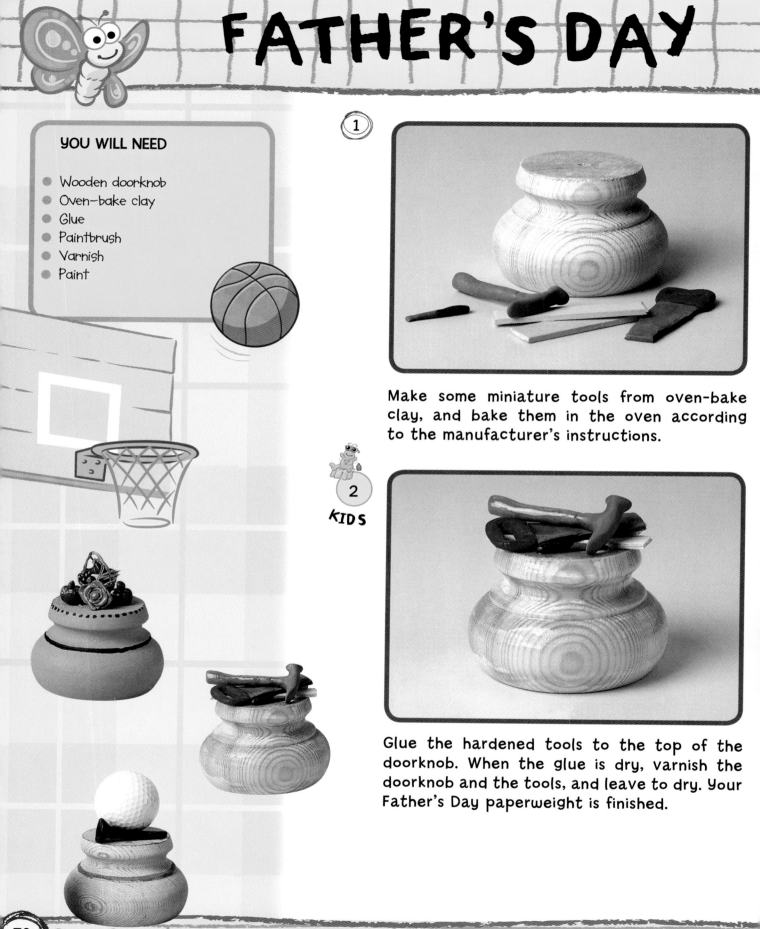

YOU WILL NEED

- Wooden doorknob
- Oven-bake clay
- Glue
- Paintbrush
- Varnish
- Paint

1

Make some miniature tools from oven-bake clay, and bake them in the oven according to the manufacturer's instructions.

2

KIDS

Glue the hardened tools to the top of the doorknob. When the glue is dry, varnish the doorknob and the tools, and leave to dry. Your Father's Day paperweight is finished.

Try out different designs. If your father loves golfing, decorate one with a golf ball and tee. You could even paint the doorknob green for the golf course.

Choose decorations that suit your father's personality or hobbies.

USA WREATH

YOU WILL NEED

- Large paper plate
- Scissors
- Pencil
- Ruler
- 1 x 4-inch strips of red and blue paper
- Adhesive tape
- White paper
- Gluestick
- Thin white ribbon
- Glitter glue (optional)

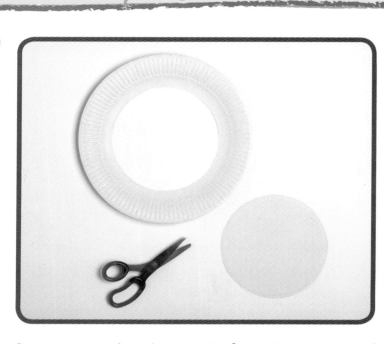

Draw and cut out a circle from the middle of the paper plate, leaving an even border all the way round, about two inches wide.

2

KIDS

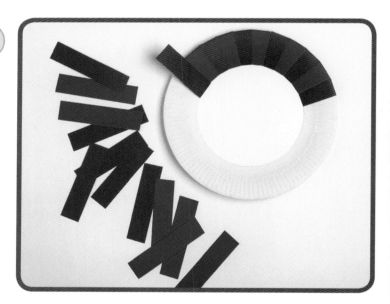

For the next step, you will need lots of strips of red and blue paper. Wrap them around the plate in stripes. Tape them on the back as you go.

③

Cut out white stars and glue them around the edge. Twist the thin white ribbon around the wreath. Secure on the back with tape.

④

Cut out a blue star, and stick a smaller white and red star in the center. Tape it to the wreath with ribbon, so it hangs down. Add a long loop of ribbon to hang up your wreath.

DID YOU KNOW?
The American flag is sometimes called the "Stars and Stripes."

You can decorate the white stars with glitter glue to make them sparkly.

DAIRY DRINKS

YOU WILL NEED

- Blender
- Fresh strawberries and bananas
- Selection of ice creams or frozen yogurts
- Low fat milk or substitute
- Whipped cream
- Sprinkles
- Low fat yogurt
- Ice chips
- Drinking straws

STRAWBERRY MILKSHAKE

1

Blend together six large strawberries, half a banana, a scoop of strawberry ice cream, and half a glass of low fat milk.

2

KIDS

Serve with sprinkles on top, and for special occasions some whipped cream.

BANANA MILKSHAKE

1

Blend together one banana, half a glass of low fat yogurt, and some ice chips. Serve in a tall glass.

CHOCOLATE MILKSHAKE

1

Blend together one small, roughly chopped banana, a large scoop of chocolate ice cream, and half a glass of milk.

For special occasions, serve with whipped cream, two or three banana slices, and chocolate sprinkles.

STRAWBERRY SMOOTHIE

Blend together six large strawberries, half a glass of strawberry yogurt, and some ice chips.

Serve in a tall glass with a blob of strawberry yogurt, a strawberry on top, and a straw.

DID YOU KNOW?
Low fat milk drinks are delicious and healthy. Milk is high in calcium; the body uses it to build strong bones.

Try sprinkling granola over the top for extra crunch and yummy flavor.

SUNDAE SPECIALS

YOU WILL NEED

- Bananas
- Strawberries
- Ice cream
- Ladyfingers or sponge biscuits
- Marshmallow spread
- Whipped cream
- Chocolate jimmies
- Strawberry jelly
- Cookies (optional)
- Strawberry syrup

BANANA AND CHOCOLATE ICE CREAM SUNDAE

1 KIDS

Put one layer at a time into the glass. Start with sliced banana, then add a spoonful of soft marshmallow spread.

2 KIDS

Sprinkle on some chocolate jimmies, then add a small scoop of vanilla ice cream. Decorate the top with whipped cream and a cookie for a special treat.

STRAWBERRY PARFAIT

Mix two teaspoons of jelly with two teaspoons of warm water. Pour over a layer of crushed Ladyfingers.

Follow with a scoop of vanilla ice cream, strawberry syrup and chopped strawberries.

Finally, decorate your creation with whipped cream and a whole strawberry.

DID YOU KNOW? The ice cream sundae was invented more than 100 years ago in the USA. Yum!

Make up your own special sundae! What will you put in it?

FRUIT POPSICLES

YOU WILL NEED

- Popsicle molds or paper cups
- Fruit juices
- Popsicle sticks
- Chopped fruit (small pieces)
- Sprinkles

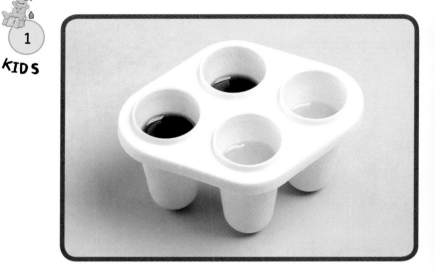

1 KIDS

Choose your favorite juices and carefully pour them into the Popsicle molds so they are half full.

2 KIDS

Put the molds in the freezer until the juice is starting to set, but isn't completely frozen. Now place the Popsicle sticks into the molds. Add some chopped fruit and top up with different flavored juices. Put the Popsicles back into the freezer to set.

③

When they are completely frozen, run the molds under a warm tap to help loosen the Popsicles before removing them.

DID YOU KNOW? Before freezers were invented, ice was a luxury!

For a special treat, add sprinkles at the bottom of the mold.

SOCK PUPPETS

YOU WILL NEED

- Clean, old sock
- Thin cardboard strip
- Scissors
- Colored felt: pink and same color as sock
- White glue
- Big black button
- 2 small white felt circles
- 2 small black buttons
- Needle and thread
- Length ribbon

Push a long strip of card inside the sock, so that it is stretched out flat. This will make it easier to work with.

2

KIDS

Cut out a long felt tongue. Dab glue at one end and stick it near the end of the sock, so it can flap about.

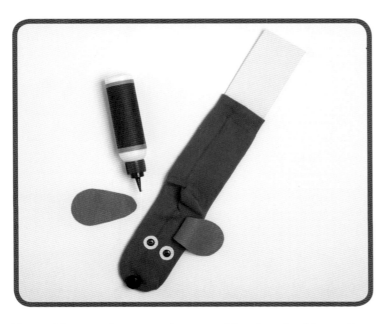

Turn the sock over. Sew on the big button for the nose. Sew or glue the small black buttons onto the white felt circles for eyes, then sew or glue them in place. Cut out two felt ears. Stick them in place, as shown.

Try to use old, odd socks – and make sure you wash them first!

Leave the puppet to dry, then tie a ribbon around the neck and secure in place with glue. What will you name your puppet?

PAPER FLOWERS

YOU WILL NEED

- Selection of tissue paper in various colors
- Pencil
- Scissors
- Florist's wire
- Glue
- Green florist's tape

1

Layer three colors of tissue paper together and draw a flower shape. Cut out.

2

Snip a small hole through the center of the paper flowers.

3

KIDS

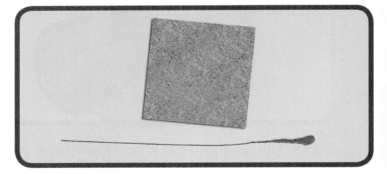

Wrap a small piece of paper around the top of some florist's wire to make the flower center and stem.

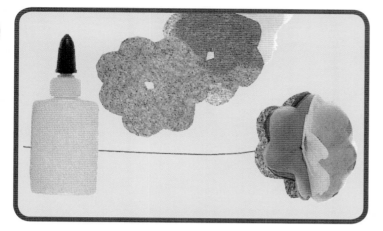

Thread the flowers on to the stem, and glue them to the flower center.

⑤

Wind some green tape around the wire to finish off the stem.

DID YOU KNOW?
More than half of the fresh-cut flowers in the USA are grown in sunny California.

Make a bouquet of flowers for a gift, or just as a pretty decoration.

BASEBALL CAPS

YOU WILL NEED

- Plain baseball cap
- Fabric paint
- Paintbrush
- Pencil
- Colored felt scraps
- Scissors
- Glue
- Sequins
- Gold thread

1 KIDS

Choose two contrasting colors and paint the side panels and brim of a baseball cap to make it striped. You may need to paint two or three coats. Leave to dry between coats.

2

Draw some shapes on the colored felt scraps, for example, butterflies, spots, or flowers, and cut them out. Practice drawing the shapes on a piece of scrap paper first, before you cut them out of the felt.

When you are happy with your felt shapes, carefully glue them onto the baseball cap, taking care not to use too much glue.

Add lots of colorful sequins and gold thread to make your cap sparkle. Leave to dry before you wear it.

DID YOU KNOW?
Baseball caps not only look great; they help protect your face from the sun.

Batter up!

PARTY HATS

YOU WILL NEED

- Thin cardboard
- Scissors
- Crêpe paper
- Needle and thread
- Glue
- Colored paper
- Glitter
- Pencil and ruler

1

Cut a band of card about three inches wide, to fit around your head with a small overlap.

2

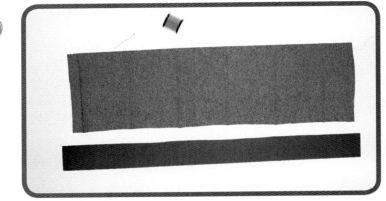

Cut a strip of crêpe paper, the same length as the band but deeper. Hand baste a line of loose stitches along the long side of the crêpe paper.

3
KIDS

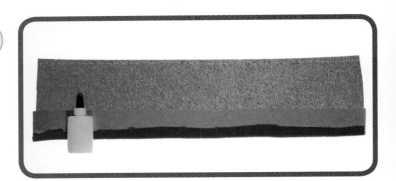

Glue the crêpe paper onto the band, with the basting at the top.

Glue the two ends of the hat band together. Pull the ends of the thread to gather the paper. Tie a knot.

5

IDS

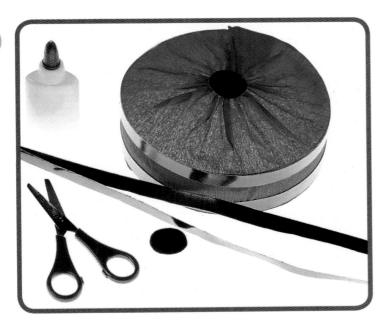

Cut out a small circle of card or paper and glue it over the center of the hat. Decorate the hat with colored paper, card, and glitter.

DID YOU KNOW?
We lose lots of body heat through our heads – so hats are good for keeping us warm.

Use glitter, sequins, colored gems, and bright ribbon to decorate your hats.

DOOR HANGERS

YOU WILL NEED

- Colored cardboard 4 x 9 inches
- Pencil
- Ruler
- Scissors
- Foam letters
- Selection of colored paper
- White glue
- Colored markers (optional)

①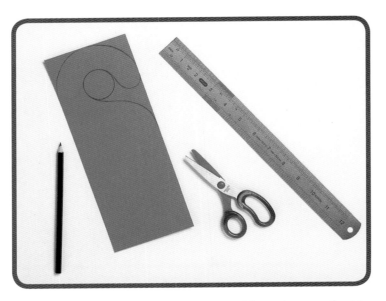

Draw a small circle near the top of the cardboard, as shown. Then draw a shape like the top of a letter "S" around the circle.

②

Carefully cut out the "S" shape with a pair of scissors, to make the basic door hanger. It is now ready to be decorated.

KEEP OUT

Use foam letters and glue to write a message on your door hanger. If you have no foam letters, write a message with colorful pens instead.

Decorate your door hanger with paper cut-outs. Look at these door hangers for ideas, then let your imagination go!

DID YOU KNOW? People hang all sorts of things on doors and doorknobs. Can you think of any?

You can decorate the other side, too!

YOU WILL NEED

- Large colored paper cup
- Scissors
- Colored paper
- Adhesive tape
- Colorful crêpe paper or tissue paper
- Two white cardboard circles
- Black marker pen
- Thread

①

Cut off the bottom of the paper cup. If the cup has writing on it, cover it with a piece of colored paper, secure it with tape or glue, and trim the edges.

② KIDS

Cut out circles of colored paper, and use them to decorate the outside of the paper cup. Stick on two white circles for eyes, adding a black dot in the middle for the pupils.

DID YOU KNOW?
Which way is the
wind blowing? Watch
the streamers on
your creature!

Cut or tear long strips of crêpe or tissue paper and tape them all the way round the inside of the cup, at the widest end.

4

Tape a long loop of thread at the top end of the cup so you can hang it up in the porch or on a tree. Watch the streamers dangle and blow in the wind!

FALL CRAFTS

LEAF PICTURES

YOU WILL NEED

- Fall leaves (different shapes and sizes)
- Heavy book (e.g. dictionary)
- White glue
- Picture frame
- Paintbrush
- Acrylic paints: black, gold
- Sponge
- Saucer

1 KIDS

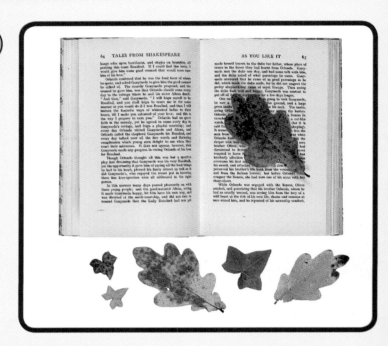

Choose some leaves with interesting shapes and colors. Place them between the pages of a heavy book. Leave them for several weeks to flatten and dry.

Arrange the dry leaves on a sheet of paper. Glue them down and ask an adult to put the paper in a frame.

To make an even more decorative picture, paint the leaves black. When dry, sponge on gold paint in patches and leave to dry.

DID YOU KNOW? The warm sunny fall days and cool fall nights make the red, orange, and yellow leaves appear even brighter.

Elmo makes leaf people. A leaf could be a body or a head. Then draw the rest of the picture around it.

PINECONE BIRDS

YOU WILL NEED

- Clean, dry pinecones
- Acrylic paints
- Paintbrush
- Pipe cleaners
- Scissors
- White glue
- Two googly eyes
- Scrap of orange cardboard
- Colored feathers (from craft shop)
- Thread

1

KIDS

Paint a pinecone in a bright color and leave to dry. Twist a colorful pipe cleaner around the middle of the pinecone to make two legs the same length.

2

Cut another pipe cleaner into lengths, three inches long. Twist the pieces around the ends of the legs to make the bird's feet, as shown.

Cut a triangular beak out of a folded piece of orange cardboard. Glue on the googly eyes and the beak. Glue feathers into the side of the cone to make the wings.

4

Tie a loop of thread to the top of the pine cone, if you wish, and hang up your bird.

DID YOU KNOW?
When wet weather is on the way, pinecones close up.

LUNCHBOXES

YOU WILL NEED

- Plastic food storage box with lid or lunchbox
- Craft foam
- Scissors
- Foam letters
- White glue or sticky foam pads
- Double-sided tap (optional)

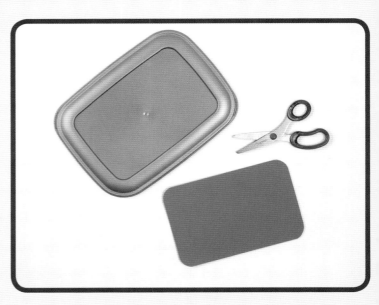

①

Cut out a rectangle of foam to fit onto the lunch box or lid of the plastic box. Round off the corners to make it look neat.

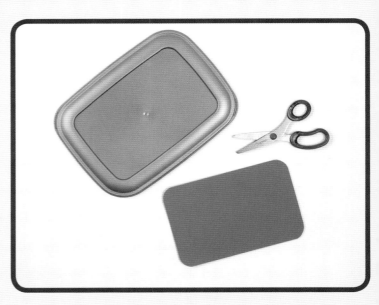

BEN

Cut out foam shapes to decorate the foam rectangle. Arrange them with some ready-cut foam letters to spell out your name. Experiment with positioning, until you are happy with your design, then glue it in place.

Cut out shapes of your favorite foods to decorate the lid.

Place the finished design onto the lid. You can use glue, but if you use sticky foam pads or double-sided tape it can easily be removed for washing or switched for another design.

IDENTITY TAGS

YOU WILL NEED

- Lid from a glass jar
- Colored cardboard
- Pencil
- Scissors
- White glue
- Craft foam
- Glitter glue
- Paper clip

1

Draw around the jar lid onto cardboard to make two identical circles. Cut them out.

2

Glue one of the circles inside the lid. Put the other circle to one side. Cut out your initial from craft foam. Make sure it will fit inside the lid. Glue it in the middle of the lid, then add some glitter glue decoration. Leave to dry.

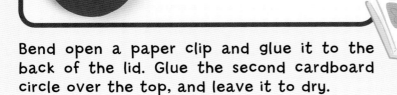

Bend open a paper clip and glue it to the back of the lid. Glue the second cardboard circle over the top, and leave it to dry.

When your bag tag is completely dry, it is ready to hang from your bag.

DID YOU KNOW?
There are twenty six letters in the English alphabet! The Russian alphabet has thirty-three!

PENCIL CASES

YOU WILL NEED

- Tall containers with tightly fitting lids, such as potato chip tubes
- Newspaper
- White glue and brush
- Scissors
- Acrylic paints
- Paintbrushes
- Glitter

Clean the container. Make sure your pens, pencils and ruler will fit inside. Glue on a layer of newspaper squares so the box is completely covered. Leave in a warm, airy spot to dry.

Paint the pencil case with a base coat, let dry, then paint on any picture or pattern you like. You could add shiny stars or glitter for decoration.

DID YOU KNOW?
Enough pencils are produced in the world every year to circle Earth 62 times!

Place a sheet of paper under your craft before sprinkling the glitter. Pour any extra glitter back into the container.

COLORED MARKER TUBS

YOU WILL NEED

- Cardboard containers
- Old newspaper
- White glue
- Acrylic paints
- Glitter
- Paintbrushes
- Scissors

1 KIDS

Glue newspaper squares onto the container so there are no gaps between the pieces. Cover the container and leave in a warm, airy place to dry.

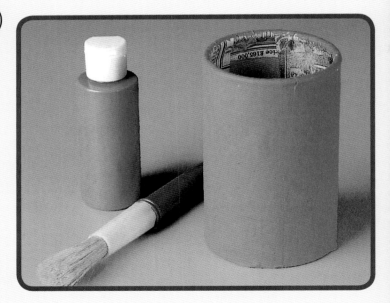

2 KIDS

Paint on a base coat and allow it to dry. You may need two coats of paint to cover it completely.

Paint on any picture you like, using one color at a time.

Me use colored gift wrap to glue around container instead of newspaper and paint.

When the paint is dry, spread glue on the areas you want to decorate, then sprinkle on glitter. Do this one color at a time and leave it to dry between colors.

CREATIVE CASES

YOU WILL NEED

- Clear plastic cases or pouches
- Black outliner
- Glass paints

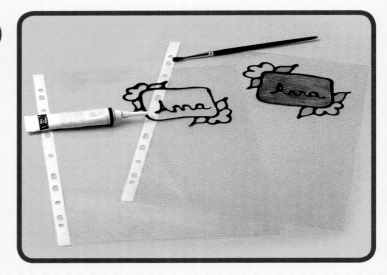

1 KIDS

Make sure that the plastic case or pouch is completely clean. Then use the black outliner to draw your design on it. Maybe draw your favorite animal or shape, or write your name. Leave the outliner to dry for at least one hour.

2 KIDS

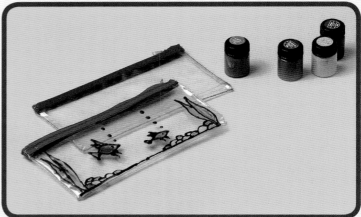

Now it's time to fill in the color on your case or pouch. Paint on each color with a clean, dry brush. Do one color at a time, making sure you clean the brush carefully between each one. When dry, your creative case or pouch is ready for colorful paper, crayons, or pens.

BOOKMARKS

YOU WILL NEED

- 2 x 6-inch long strips thin cardboard
- Pencil
- Scissors
- Colored marker pens

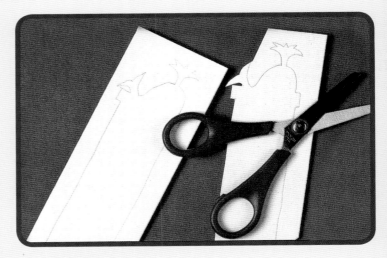

This picture shows you how to make a whale bookmark, but you can choose any design you like. Use your pencil to outline a whale (or whatever design you choose) on top of a long rectangular shape. When you are happy with the shape cut it out.

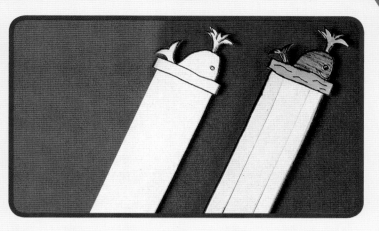

Use markers to color in the design, then carefully give it an outline with a black marker.

3

You can personalize your bookmark by using your initial. Draw it in pencil first. Give it an outline with a black marker when you decorate it.

4

This bookmark would look good in a gardening book.

DID YOU KNOW?
English has more words than most languages. And thousands of new words are added every year!

Mmm. Delicious!

NAME T-SHIRTS

YOU WILL NEED

- Craft foam
- Pencil
- Ruler
- Scissors
- Plain T-shirt
- Thick cardboard
- Fabric paints
- Sponge

①

Draw out the letters of your name on some craft foam. Try to make sure they are all the same size. Cut them out.

②

Push a large piece of cardboard inside the T-shirt, to stop paint from soaking through. Position the letters, and draw around them in pencil. One at a time, sponge paint over the back of the letters, and press them down in position on the T-shirt.

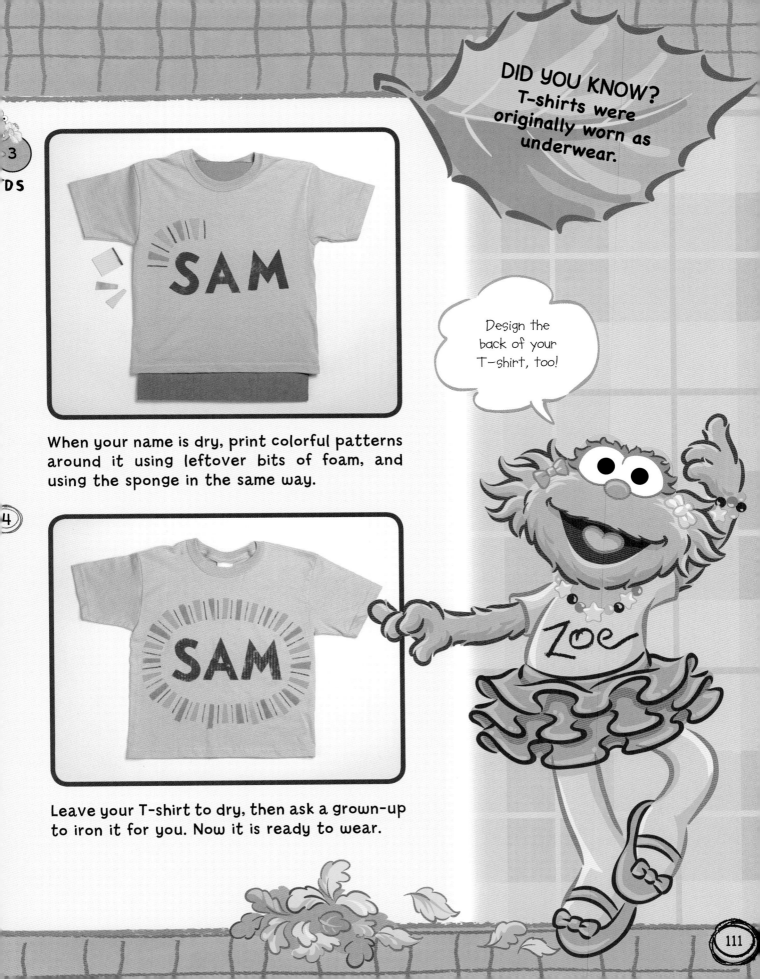

DID YOU KNOW?
T-shirts were originally worn as underwear.

Design the back of your T-shirt, too!

When your name is dry, print colorful patterns around it using leftover bits of foam, and using the sponge in the same way.

Leave your T-shirt to dry, then ask a grown-up to iron it for you. Now it is ready to wear.

EID DECORATIONS

YOU WILL NEED

- Paper plate
- Pencil
- Scissors
- Aluminum foil
- White glue and brush
- Glitter
- Glittery thread

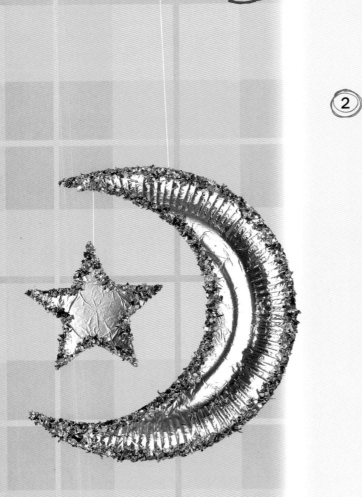

①

Draw a crescent moon and a star onto a paper plate. Cut them out.

②

Cut out pieces of foil slightly bigger than the moon and star. Cover the moon and star with foil, neatly folding in the edges as shown.

Hang your moon and star by an open window, so it can twirl and sparkle in the breeze.

Brush glue all along the edges of the moon and star, then sprinkle with glitter. Leave to dry.

4

Use glittery thread to hang the star from the moon, as shown. Tie a longer thread to the top of the moon, so it can be hung from the ceiling.

PUMPKIN FUN!

YOU WILL NEED

- Pumpkin (any size)
- Black marker pen
- Knife
- Tealight

 KIDS

1 Use a black marker pen to draw a face onto one side of your pumpkin. You can draw triangles for the eyes and nose, and a jagged strip for the mouth, if you like.

2 Ask an adult to cut a circle around the top of the pumpkin for the lid, and the holes for the eyes, nose, and mouth.

3 Place a tealight inside the pumpkin so it can shine through the holes. Ask a grown-up to light it for you.

DID YOU KNOW? Halloween is a holiday celebrated each year on October 31. Children dress up in costumes for fun and get treats.

Remember to say "thank you" each time you get a Halloween treat!

115

MAKING INK

YOU WILL NEED

- Dark-colored fruit and vegetables, and daffodil petals
- Pestle and mortar
- Jar
- Water
- Piece of cheesecloth
- Lemon
- Paper and dipping pen

Crush dark-colored fruit such as cherries, raspberries, or cranberries in a pestle and mortar to make juice. Strain the juice into a jar through the cheesecloth, and throw the fruit pulp away. Now put the nib of a dipping pen into the juice, and use it to write. You can even make yellow ink from crushed daffodil petals and a little water.

Experiment with different fruit, vegetables, and flower petals to discover which ones work the best.

You can use lemon juice to make invisible ink. Squeeze the juice of half a lemon into a small jar. Use a dipping pen or a thin paintbrush to write your invisible message on a sheet of paper. Leave it to dry. To make the writing visible you will need to ask a grown-up to iron it. Watch as the heat from the iron turns your invisible message brown.

HARVEST SUPPER

YOU WILL NEED

- Knife
- Large saucepan and water
- Fork
- Small soup bowls
- Ladle

Ingredients:
- 1 onion
- 2 sticks of celery
- 2 medium potatoes
- 2 large carrots
- 1 leek
- Vegetable stock cube
- 1 teaspoon mixed herbs
- 1 tablespoon tomato paste
- Salt and pepper (to taste)

1

Chop up the vegetables, then place all the ingredients into a saucepan and cover them with water. Bring the soup to the boil, then turn down the heat so it cooks gently for half an hour.

2

KIDS

Season the soup with a pinch of salt and pepper. Ask a grown-up to check that it is cool enough, then use a ladle to serve the soup in bowls.

WINTER CRAFTS

NAPKIN RINGS

YOU WILL NEED

- Cardboard tube
- Scissors
- Pencil or marker pen
- White glue and brush
- Tissue paper strips
- Foil candy wrappers torn into strips

1

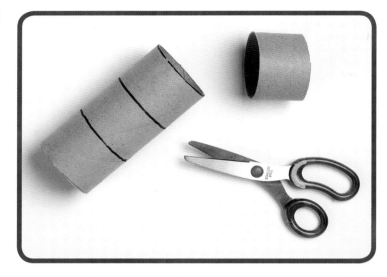

Mark sections about one inch wide on the cardboard tube, as shown, then carefully cut the tube into sections.

2
KIDS

Brush glue all over the outside and inside of each ring. Wrap tissue paper strips around them, brushing on more glue to help them stick. Glue foil strips over the tissue strips for a sparkly effect.

Touch up with glue in spots that need it, then leave to dry. Roll up a napkin and push it into a ring, then put at table setting.

DID YOU KNOW?
Long ago, instead of using napkins, people wiped their hands on a slice of bread.

Napkins are handy for sticky desserts!

MENORAH CANDLES

YOU WILL NEED

- Pack air-drying clay
- Modeling tool
- Rolling pin
- Pencil
- Acrylic paints
- Paintbrush
- Glitter
- Candles (birthday cake candles work well)

①

Divide the clay in half. Roll out one half into a long rectangle, about one inch thick. Cut a zigzag along one edge for the base of the menorah. Flatten all the points slightly so that it will stand up. Then use the modeling tool to cut the base into three sections: two with four points, and one with two points.

②
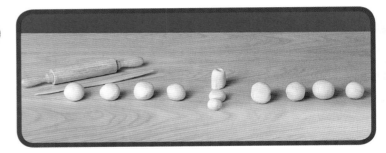

Divide up the remaining clay into balls. Roll eleven into short sausage shapes for the candleholders—three for the center and four on each side. Make holes for the candles with a pencil.

3

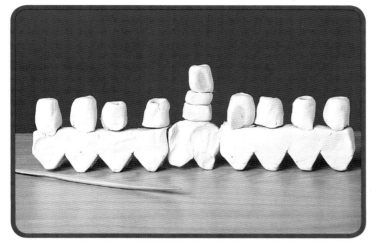

Use the modeling tool to assemble the menorah. Leave it to dry in a warm, airy place before decorating it.

4

KIDS

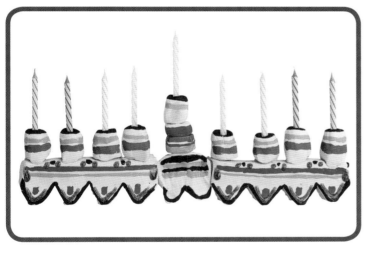

Decorate the menorah with paint and glitter, and let dry. Ask an adult to help you use it during the eight nights of Hanukkah. The center, or leader, candle, is used to light one more candle each night, until they are all lit on the last night.

DID YOU KNOW?
Hanukkah is the Jewish Festival of Lights. It lasts for eight days and nights in the wintertime.

KWANZAA HAT

YOU WILL NEED

- Thin cardboard: black, green, red
- Scissors
- Pencil
- Ruler
- Glue or adhesive tape

①

Cut a strip of thin black cardboard two inches wide by twenty-four inches long. Cut a thinner strip of green cardboard the same length. Decorate by gluing bits of red and black paper on the green strip.

② KIDS

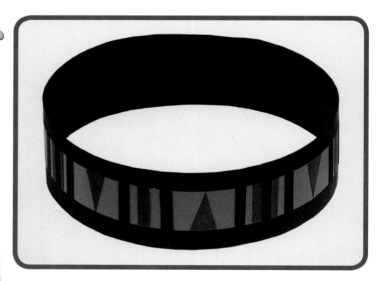

Glue the green strip in the middle of the black strip, as shown. Overlap the ends of the band and tape them together to fit around your head.

Cut three red and three green strips, one inch wide by twelve inches long. Bend one of them across the inside of the headband and stick down both ends.

4
DS

Do the same with the other five strips, so they are evenly spaced as shown. Cut out a small round circle and glue it on the top to finish your Kwanzaa hat.

DID YOU KNOW?
Kwanzaa is a week-long African-American holiday in December. It celebrates family, community, and culture.

Hey!
I'm Kwanzaa-colored!
Now scram!

CHRISTMAS COOKIES

YOU WILL NEED

- Wooden spoon
- Large bowl
- Whisk
- Sieve
- Rolling pin
- Shaped cookie cutters
- Baking sheet
- Cooling rack

- 1 stick butter
- ½ cup sugar
- 1 egg
- 1 teaspoon baking spice
- 1 cup flour

Icing and decoration:
- ½ cup confectioner's sugar
- 1–4 tablespoons hot water
- Tubes of colored icing
- Jimmies to decorate

①

Cream the butter and sugar with a wooden spoon until light and fluffy, then whisk in the egg. Sift in the rest of the ingredients and mix together to make a firm dough. Cover with plastic wrap and chill for two hours.

②

Roll out the dough on a lightly floured surface to about a quarter of an inch thick. Cut out Christmas shapes. Place the shapes onto a greased baking sheet. Bake in a pre-heated oven at 375°F for ten minutes until golden brown.

3
IDS

While the cookies are cooling, mix the confectioner's sugar with a little hot water and a few drops of food coloring. When cool, ice, then decorate the cookies using jimmies and tubes of colored icing.

4
IDS

When the icing is set, serve the cookies on a plate. Delicious!

DID YOU KNOW?
Traditional German Christmas cookies contain delicious spices such as ginger and cinnamon.

Me love holiday cookies! Num-num!

COOKIES

PAPER SNOWFLAKES

YOU WILL NEED

- Small paper plate
- Pencil
- Scissors
- White glue and brush
- Glitter: silver, gold, white
- Thread

1 KIDS

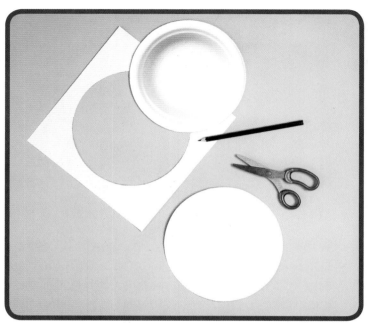

Trace around a small plate onto a piece of white paper. Cut out the circle.

2

Fold the circle in half three times, so you end up with a triangle shape. Draw a snowflake pattern along the folded edges of the triangle. Cut out the pattern, making sure you don't cut all the way through the folded edges.

S

Carefully unfold your snowflake. Cover one side with glue and sprinkle it all over with glitter. Shake off any loose glitter onto scrap paper, and keep it to use for the other side of your snowflake. Let dry.

4

Cover the other side of the snowflake in glue and glitter. When the glue and glitter are completely dry, tie some thread through a hole in the top to hang it up.

DID YOU KNOW?
No two snowflakes are exactly the same, but every real snowflake has six points.

Catch a snowflake on your tongue. It tickles!

QUIET CRACKERS

YOU WILL NEED

- Cardboard tubes
- Tissue or crêpe paper rectangles (3 times as long as tubes and wide enough to overlap)
- White glue and brush
- Adhesive tape
- Foil and colorful paper
- Candies, small gifts, and confetti

Place a cardboard tube in the middle of a large rectangle of tissue or crêpe paper.

Roll the paper around the tube, secure it with tape, then twist it at one end to close it. Push candies, confetti, and a small gift into the tube.

Twist the other end of the cracker to close it, then decorate the cracker with festive decorations.

Make a lot of different colored crackers, one for each guest at your holiday party. You could even put a name on each one.

DID YOU KNOW?
The first crackers were just like the ones here, but later, the inventor added a loud POP!

You could also write your favorite jokes on small strips of paper, and put one in each cracker.

POM-POM SNOWMAN

YOU WILL NEED

- Cardboard tube
- 5 sheets old newspaper
- Cotton batting
- Adhesive tape
- Marker pen
- Glue
- Small black buttons
- Orange felt
- Old, clean sock
- Ribbon

1

Twist some sheets of newspaper as shown, then tape them around the cardboard tube to make the snowman's body.

2

Keep adding layers of newspaper until you have a rounded body shape. Roll a newspaper ball for the head.

3
KIDS

Brush glue over the head and body, cover with batting.

Glue the head on the body. Glue on a ribbon scarf, two small matching buttons for eyes, and a felt nose.

5

Cut the end off a sock to make a hat to keep your snowman warm. Glue three small matching buttons down his front, and add a friendly smile to finish.

DID YOU KNOW?
The biggest snowflake ever recorded was fifteen inches in diameter!

Make sure you ask a grown-up's permission first, before you cut up any socks!

FESTIVE STOCKINGS

1

Draw a stocking shape on cardboard and cut it out. Lay the shape on two pieces of felt, then trace around it and cut out two felt shapes.

2

KIDS

Glue around the edges of the two felt stockings, leaving the top edge unglued so the top stays open. Press the two sides together. Leave to dry.

Decorate your stocking with festive felt shapes. Add sequins, gold ribbon, and craft gems for extra sparkle.

4

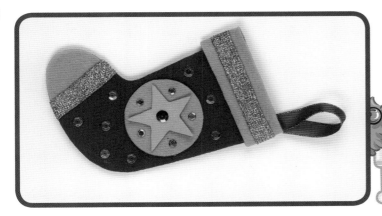

Glue a loop of red ribbon to the inside of your stocking at the back, so you can hang it up.

DID YOU KNOW?
In some countries, children leave their shoes, not stockings, to be filled with treats.

Try using glitter on your stocking, too. Sparkalicious!

FINGER PUPPETS

YOU WILL NEED

- Clean, old glove
- Scissors
- Cardboard strips
- Colored felt
- Glue or double-sided tape
- Pipe cleaners
- Colored wool
- Colored beads
- Sequins and ribbon scraps

1 Cut the fingers off an old glove. Try to cut each one the same size. Push a strip of cardboard inside each finger, to make it easier to work.

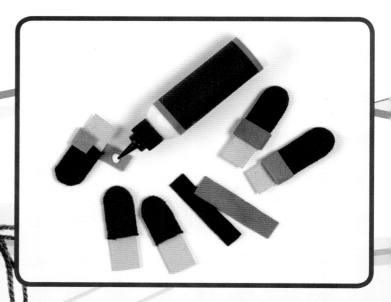

2 Cut strips of felt, and glue them around the bottom ends of the fingers as shown, to stop them from fraying.

Push a pipe cleaner through the top of the glove fingers, so that the two ends stick out. Curl each end around a pencil to make curly antennae. To make hair, tie strands of wool together.

4
DS

Glue on the hair, and add beads for the eyes and nose. Then decorate your finger puppets with sequins and scraps of ribbon to finish them off.

DID YOU KNOW?
A marionette is a puppet with strings to make it move.

REINDEER PUPPET

YOU WILL NEED

- Clean wooden spoon
- Acrylic paint: brown
- Paintbrush
- Brown cardboard
- Felt
- Scissors
- White glue
- Two googly eyes
- Small red pom-pom
- Brown wool
- Gold ribbon

KIDS

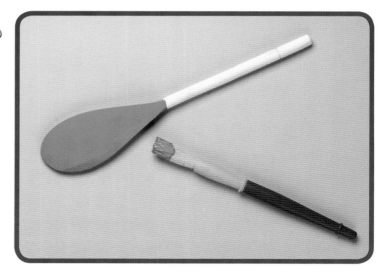

Paint the top of a wooden spoon brown, and leave it to dry.

Fold some brown cardboard in half. Draw an antler shape on one side, then cut it out to make two matching antlers. Cut out two felt ears, as shown.

Glue the antlers and ears to the back of the spoon, as shown. Then glue the two googly eyes and the red pom-pom nose in place. Leave to dry.

4

Snip some short lengths of wool, and glue between the antlers to give your reindeer hair. Tie the gold ribbon around the neck to finish your reindeer puppet.

GIFT BOXES

YOU WILL NEED

- Paper or thin cardboard (letter size will make a box approx. 3 inches square)
- Ruler and pencil
- Scissors
- White glue
- Hole punch
- Colored ribbon
- Double-sided tape
- Self-adhesive stickers (optional)

1 KIDS Fold a rectangular piece of paper in half.

2 Fold each half in on itself, so that both ends meet in the middle.

3 KIDS With the paper opened out, you will see crease marks like this.

4 KIDS Now fold the paper into thirds in the opposite direction to your first folds. It should look like this picture when you finish with 12 folded squares.

⑤

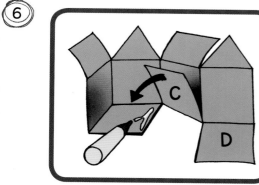

Carefully cut up along the creases marked A, B, C, D in the picture above. Make sure you do not cut beyond the crease of the bottom squares. Then snip off the corners of the top squares of B and D to make triangles as shown above.

⑥

Fold in and glue flap B onto flap A, flap C onto flap B and flap D onto flap C.

⑦

Place double-sided tape on the inside of the open edge to close. Make a hole at the top of both triangles for a ribbon with the hole punch. Decorate your box.

Elmo likes to tie a bow around the box!

143

CHRISTMAS TREE CARDS

YOU WILL NEED

- Sheet green paper or thin cardboard
- Black marker pen
- Scissors
- Scraps red paper
- Gluestick
- Colored star sequins
- 3 large gold star sequins

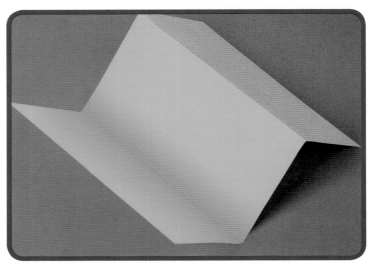

Fold the sheet of green paper or cardboard in three, as shown.

Draw the outline of a Christmas tree and pot. Make sure the branches run off at the fold or the card will fall apart when you cut it out. Fold the card up and cut the tree out.

Cut three pot shapes from the red paper and glue to the card.

Glue the gold stars to the top of each tree. Add sequins all over the trees to decorate them and let dry.

DID YOU KNOW?
Christmas trees are evergreen. That means they do not lose their leaves, or needles, in winter.

Oh boy! I love sending holiday cards. Who will you send yours to?

GIFT TAGS

YOU WILL NEED

- Thin, colored cardboard
- Colored construction paper
- Ruler
- Pencil
- Scissors
- Hole punch
- Gluestick
- Ribbon: red, green

Measure and cut out some cardboard rectangles six inches by four inches. Fold them in half to make tags, and press along the fold line. Punch holes in the corners, as shown.

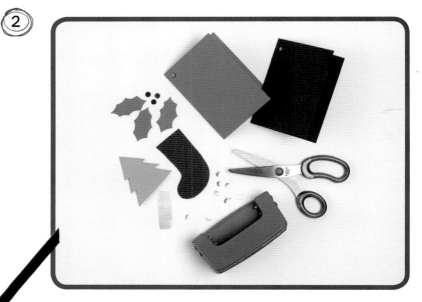

Draw some Christmas decorations onto construction paper and cut them out. Use the hole punch to make lots of circles in different colors out of leftover bits of paper.

Glue the decorations and hole-punch circles onto the front of the folded tags. Thread ribbon through the holes, so you can attach your tags to gifts.

DID YOU KNOW? Holidays are a great time to get in touch with friends and family.

A grown-up can help you write the name of someone special.

GIFT WRAP

YOU WILL NEED

- Paper
- Pencil and marker pen
- Scissors
- Tissue paper (to fit gift)
- Paint: gold
- Old saucer
- Sponge
- Hole punch
- Thread
- Clothespins

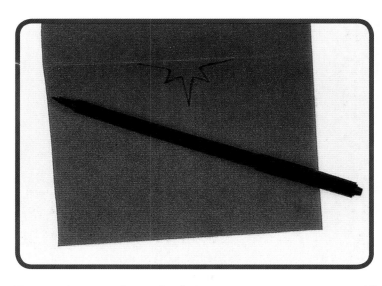

To make a stencil, fold some paper in half and draw half of a star along the fold line, as shown in the picture.

Use the scissors to cut the shape out, taking care not to leave any jagged edges. Try not to cut into the paper, too. If you do, the stencil paint may come through.

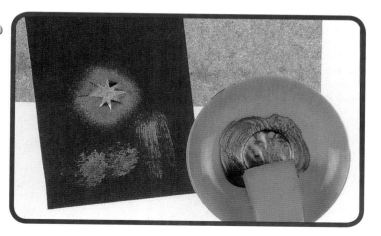

Lay out the sheet of tissue paper on a clean work surface. Pour a little paint into a saucer, dip the sponge in, then dab it on paper to get rid of extra paint. Practice stenciling on rough paper, until you are confident.

Stencil the shape all over the tissue paper, taking care not to smudge the paint when you lift the stencil off the paper. Hang up your stenciled paper with clothespins on a line to dry. It is a good idea to make a few sheets at a time.

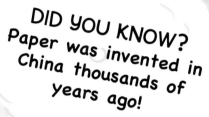

DID YOU KNOW?
Paper was invented in China thousands of years ago!

Me want to make stencil cookies.

CHINESE NEW YEAR

YOU WILL NEED

- Thin cardboard 10 x 8 inches
- Colored markers
- Glitter
- White glue and brush
- Scissors
- Tissue paper (cut into thin strips)
- Colored paper (2 colors)
- Adhesive tape
- Two sticks

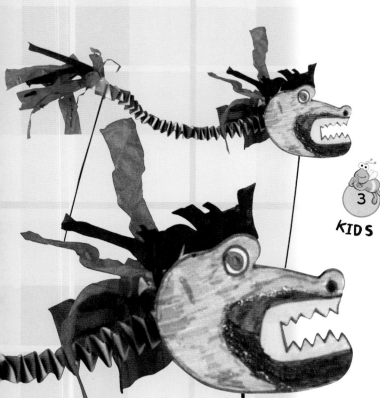

①

Draw a dragon's head onto thin cardboard. Use colored markers to color it in, then decorate it using glue and glitter.

②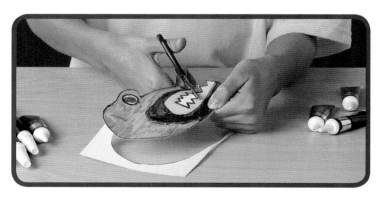

Carefully cut out the dragon's head.

③ **KIDS**

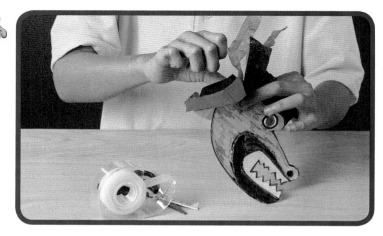

Tape half the strips of tissue paper to the back of the dragon's head.

(4)

Cut two long, thin strips of colored paper the same length. Glue one to the other to make an "L" shape. Fold the yellow strip over the top of the pink strip and crease it. Then fold the pink strip down over the yellow. Continue until you can glue down the final fold.

5

IDS

Glue the rest of the tissue paper to the dragon's tail. Glue the head to the other end of the body.

(6)

Use tape to attach the two sticks to the body – one at the head end, the other at the tail end.

DID YOU KNOW?
Chinese New Year is celebrated with a big parade. At the end of it, a dragon dances to the sound of drums, horns, and gongs!

Chinese New Year is a SUPER holiday!

VALENTINE COOKIES

YOU WILL NEED

- Large mixing bowl
- Wooden spoon
- Rolling pin
- Heart-shaped cookie cutter
- Baking sheet
- Plastic wrap
- 2⅓ cups flour
- 1 teaspoon baking powder
- 1 teaspoon vanilla
- 1 stick margarine
- 1 cup soft brown sugar
- 3 tablespoons light corn syrup
- 1 egg
- Frosting
- Candy hearts and sprinkles (optional)

1 Place the flour, baking powder, vanilla, and sugar in a bowl. Add the margarine. Mix with your fingertips until the mixture is crumbly.

2 Add the syrup; mix together. Stir in the egg and mix. Turn out the mixture onto a lightly floured surface and knead it until it forms a smooth dough. Cover with plastic wrap and chill for two hours.

Roll out the dough on a floured surface to about one quarter of an inch. Cut out the cookies with a heart-shaped cutter. Place them on a greased baking sheet and bake at 325°F for 10 minutes. Ask an adult to help you use the oven.

When the cookies are done, have an adult take them out of the oven. Leave to stand. They will harden up as they cool. When they are cool, decorate the cookies with frosting, and add some candy hearts if you wish.

DID YOU KNOW? Valentine's Day is a great time to show people you care.

Elmo uses food coloring to make pink and red frosting. Elmo thinks these are the foods of love!

LET IT RAIN CRAFTS

TOY CARS

YOU WILL NEED

- Thin colored cardboard
- Pencil and ruler
- Scissors
- Masking tape
- Acrylic paint
- Paintbrushes
- 4 bottle or juice carton lids
- 2 drinking straws
- Modeling clay

1 Draw two side views of a car on cardboard and a long thin rectangular strip to fit over the top.

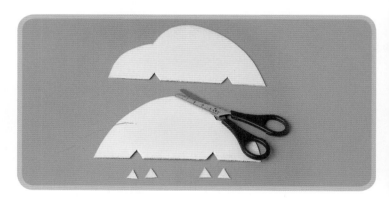

2 Cut the pieces out. Now cut out two small v-shapes in the same place on both shapes. This is where the wheels will be.

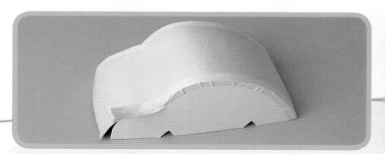

3 Use masking tape to fix the long rectangle to the top of the car sides, joining them together as shown. Then measure and cut a rectangle of cardboard to fit the bottom of the car.

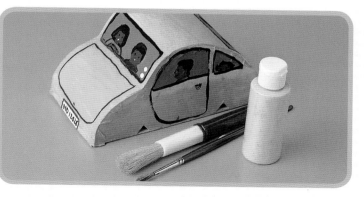

Paint the two side views and the rectangular piece that goes over the top.

Stick a ball of modeling clay to the inside of each lid and push one end of the straw into the clay.

6

Push one straw all the way through the v-shape and attach the second wheel on the other side with modeling clay. Repeat with the second straw. Your car is now finished.

DID YOU KNOW?
The first cars didn't have steering wheels. Drivers steered them with a lever.

Elmo loves cars!
Vroom, vroom!

JUGGLING BAGS

YOU WILL NEED

- Patterned fabric
- Scissors
- Uncooked lentils or other dried beans
- Needle and thread
- Spoon

1 Cut a rectangle of fabric and fold it in half, inside out. Sew seams along the side edges.

2 Turn the material right side out, ready to fill the bag.

3 KIDS

Use a spoon to half-fill the bag with the lentils or beans.

4

Neatly fold in the edges and sew them together firmly. Repeat to make more bags.

DID YOU KNOW?
Juggling is fun and healthy. It's good for the heart, and helps you learn to concentrate.

Juggling not easy, so keep practicing!

BOWLING

YOU WILL NEED

- 6 or 10 large empty plastic drink bottles
- Acrylic paints
- Paintbrushes
- Sand

1 KIDS

Carefully wash out the bottles. When they are completely dry, screw on the lids tightly.

2 KIDS

Give each container a colorful base coat. You may need to paint each one with two or more layers of paint to cover it completely. Leave to dry.

3 KIDS

Now it's time to decorate your bowling pins. Paint on patterns and shapes in different colors. When all your bottles are painted, decorated, and dry, they are ready to use.

DID YOU KNOW?
People have played bowling games since the days of ancient Egypt.

Stand the bottles in a triangle shape, as shown in the picture. If you are using six bottles, place one at the front, two in the middle, and three in the back row. Use a small ball to play your bowling game. If they are too easy to knock over, fill them with a little sand to make them heavier.

toys

FISHING GAME

YOU WILL NEED

- Dinner plate
- Thick blue cardboard
- Scissors
- Thin cardboard: blue, white
- Ruler and pencil
- Glue or adhesive tape
- Colored markers
- Colored adhesive tape (optional)
- Paper clips
- Garden stakes or other long sticks
- String

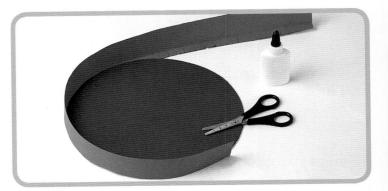

Draw around a plate on a piece of thick cardboard. Cut out the circle to make the base of the pond. Cut a long strip of thin cardboard to fit around the edge of the base and glue or tape it in place.

2 KIDS

Use colored tape or colored markers to decorate the sides.

3 KIDS

Draw ten fish and starfish on cardboard and cut them out. Decorate them with colored markers.

4

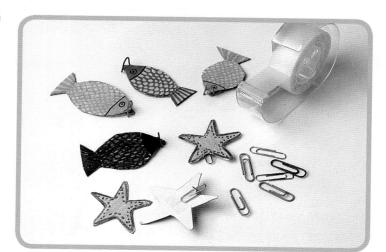

To add the loops to your cardboard fish, fold up the middle section of the paper clips and tape them to the back.

DID YOU KNOW?
The whale shark is as big as a whale, but it's not a whale. It's the biggest fish in the ocean.

Make lots of different sea creatures, such as fish, starfish, an octopus, or a crab.

5

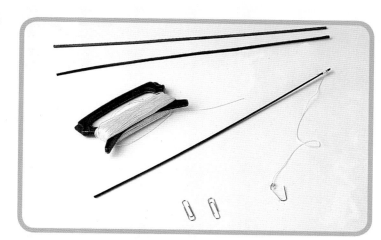

The fishing rods are made from garden stakes. Tie a paper clip to the end of a piece of string, then tape the string to the end of a garden stake. Shape the paper clip into a hook. Now you can go fishing!

AQUARIUM

YOU WILL NEED

- Large shoe box and lid
- Scissors
- Acrylic paints and paintbrush
- Sheet of plastic wrap (blue if available)
- White glue
- Advesive tape
- Green tissue paper
- Pebbles
- Thin cardboard and paper
- Colored markers
- Glitter
- Gold thread
- Self-adhesive stars (optional)

1

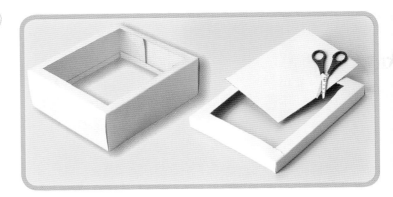

Cut a rectangle out of the box lid and the base of the box.

2

Paint the box and lid blue, inside and out.

3

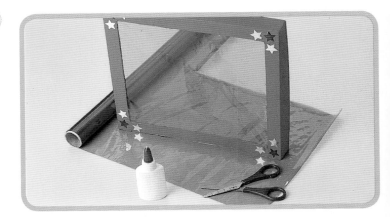

Glue a sheet of plastic wrap over the cut-out spaces.

4

Cut tissue paper strips for the weeds. Tape them to the aquarium roof so they dangle down. Lay pebbles on the bottom.

5

Draw fish on the thin cardboard and decorate them with paint and glitter.

6

Attach them to the roof with gold thread, then glue the lid on. Decorate with stars if you wish.

DID YOU KNOW?
Public aquariums can be enormous, with tanks the size of a football field!

165

PICK-UP STICKS

YOU WILL NEED

- 25 thin wooden sticks
- Colored markers

1 KIDS

1 KIDS

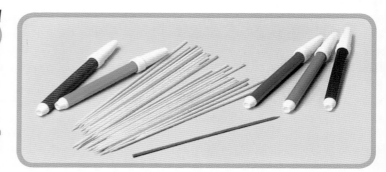

Divide the sticks into four groups of six, leaving one left over. This is the "pick-up stick." Color it in one color all over.

2 KIDS

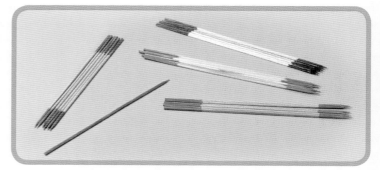

Choose a different color for each of the four groups of sticks. Color just the ends of the sticks with the coloring pens.

3 KIDS

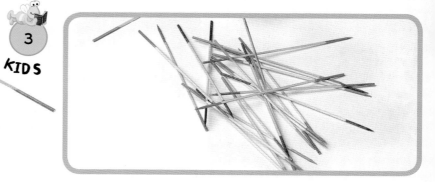

Throw the sticks onto the playing area. Use the pick-up stick to pick up a stick without moving the others. If you nudge one, it's the next player's turn. The winner is the person who picks up the most sticks.

CANDY CUSHIONS

YOU WILL NEED

- Muslin fabric or cheesecloth
- Scissors
- Wax crayons
- Needle and thread
- Greaseproof paper
- Polyester stuffing
- Iron

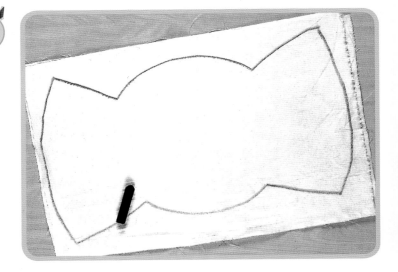

1 KIDS

Fold the fabric in half to make a double layer. Using a crayon, draw on a large wrapped candy shape to one side.

2 KIDS

Use the wax crayons to draw bright patterns on your candy shape and color them in.

3

Cut around the outside of the candy and turn them right-sides-in. Sew the two pieces together, leaving a gap for the stuffing.

4

Turn the cushion cover right-side-out. Ask a grown-up to iron it between sheets of greaseproof paper to seal the colored wax. Stuff the cushion with polyester stuffing, then sew up the gap with a needle and thread, neatly folding in the edges.

DID YOU KNOW?
Long ago, cushions were stuffed with straw—but they weren't very comfortable!

DOLLHOUSE

YOU WILL NEED

- Two shoe boxes of same size
- Scissors
- Tape and glue
- Large paper clips
- Paint and paintbrushes
- Paper and cardboard
- Small boxes
- Colored markers

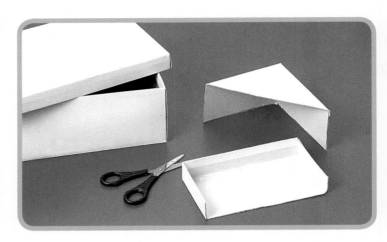

1

Use one of the shoe boxes to make the house. Cut a corner off the other box to make the roof.

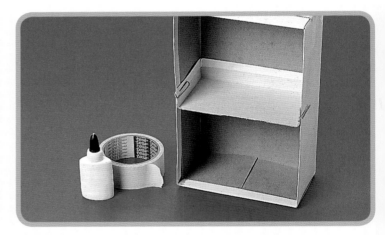

2

Cut one box lid so that it fits inside the house as the upstairs floor. Use glue and tape to stick the floor section into place. Hold the floor in position with the large paper clips while the glue is setting.

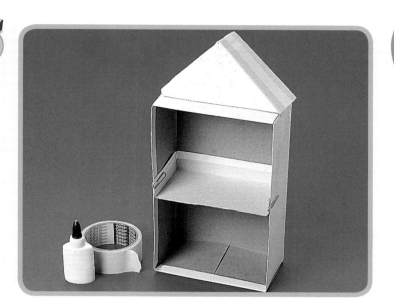

Use tape to attach the roof piece to the top of the house, as shown. Make sure you leave enough room at the front for the lid to fit.

Make the front of the house from the other shoe box lid. Cut out squares for the windows, then paint the roof and walls. Decorate the inside of your dollhouse. Use colored paper for wallpaper, fabric to make rugs, and small boxes for furniture.

DID YOU KNOW?
Queen Mary of England's dollhouse had working lights and elevators, and even flushing toilets!

CLOTH DOLL

YOU WILL NEED

- Fabric in a flesh color
- Colored marker
- Scissors
- Needle and thread
- Polyester stuffing
- Patterned fabric
- Fabric paint
- Paintbrush
- Wool
- Cardboard 3 x 3 inches
- Ribbon

1 Draw a doll shape onto a double layer of fabric.

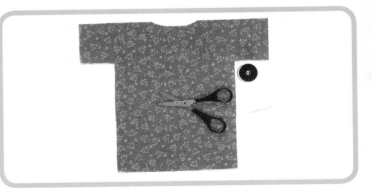

2 Sew around the drawn line, leaving an extra half inch gap to turn the fabric out. Fill it with stuffing, then cut out the doll.

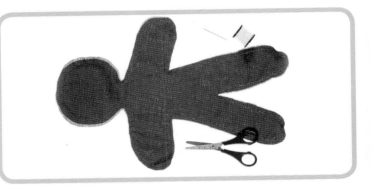

3 Draw a dress on the patterned fabric. Cut out and sew the edges together, inside out, leaving the neck, bottom, and the sleeve ends open.

4

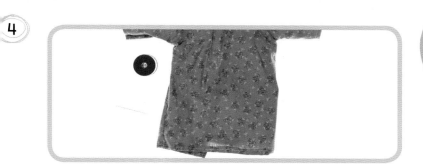

Turn the dress the right way out and sew a hem along the bottom of the fabric.

5

Paint the doll's face, then make her hair by winding the wool around a piece of cardboard and sewing a line down the middle for a "part." Attach the hair with glue.

6

KIDS

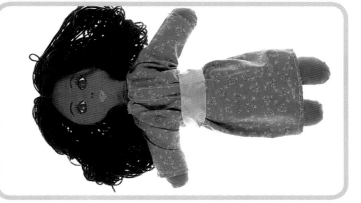

Dress your doll and tie a ribbon belt around her waist.

DID YOU KNOW?
Before the word doll was invented, people called dolls "puppets" or "babies."

You can also use the fabric shape in step 1 to make a gingerbread man shape. Then you can decorate him!

PAPER DOLL BEARS

YOU WILL NEED

- Thin cardboard
- Paper
- Pencil
- Wax crayons or pencils
- Sheets of white paper
- Scissors

1

KIDS

Draw a teddy bear onto cardboard. Give it a face and color it in.

2

Cut out the bear with scissors. Make as many bears as you want in this way.

Lay the cut-out teddy bears onto the white paper and draw an outfit around each one. Draw tabs on each outfit as shown, color in the outfits, then cut them out.

Dress your teddy bears in their new outfits, by folding back the tabs behind the bears.

DID YOU KNOW?
The teddy bear was named after American President Theodore Roosevelt.

STENCIL TOY BOX

YOU WILL NEED

- Big box
- White glue and brush
- Old newspaper
- Acrylic paints and paintbrush
- 1 sheet white paper and pencil
- Scissors
- Sponge
- Small plate
- Adhesive tape

1 KIDS

Glue two layers of newspaper inside and outside the box, covering it completely. Do this in stages, allowing the box to dry in a warm, airy place between each layer.

2 KIDS

When the layers are completely dry, paint the box. You may need two or three coats of paint to cover the newspaper completely. Remember to let the paint dry between coats.

3

Draw a simple stencil design onto the center of a sheet of paper and cut it out. You may want to make a few stencils with different shapes.

4

Loosely tape the stencil to the side of the box. Dip the sponge in a little paint and pat it on the plate to get rid of any extra, then dab it over the stencil. Practice on scrap paper before decorating your toy box.

DID YOU KNOW?
Keeping your toys in a toy box is a great way to keep them from getting broken!

CHECKERBOARD

YOU WILL NEED

- Shoe box lid
- Acrylic paints and paintbrushes
- Thin strip of craft wood (long enough to go around the cardboard rectangle)
- Pencil
- Ruler
- Scissors
- Glue
- Small box
- 16 buttons in 2 different colors (8 of each color)

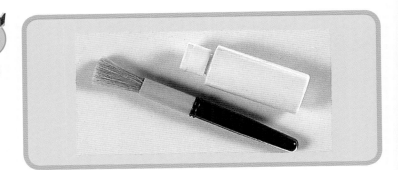

Paint the shoe box lid white to make the base of the game board, then paint the edging strip of craft wood in a darker color. Leave to dry.

2

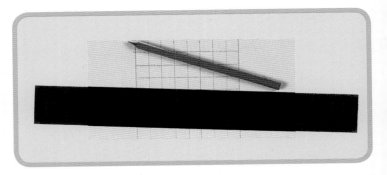

Use a ruler to measure and mark out the game board with eight rows of eight squares. Leave space at each end of the board for your pieces.

3

When you've drawn the squares, paint every other square a darker color, as shown.

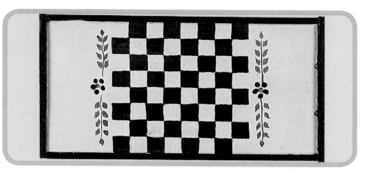

Cut the wooden edging strip into four pieces and glue in place to form the board edges. Decorate the board at each end, if you wish.

Paint a small box in the darker color and decorate it to match your game board. Use this box to store your checkers. Each player will need eight checkers. Make sure each set of checkers is a different color.

DID YOU KNOW?
An eight square board can be used to play lots of games, including chess.

Why not make your own checkers from painted pebbles if you like?

GUESSING BOX

YOU WILL NEED

- Large shoe box
- Circular object to draw around
- Marker pen
- Scissors
- Acrylic paints
- Paintbrush
- Adhesive tape
- Piece of fabric
- Glitter glue

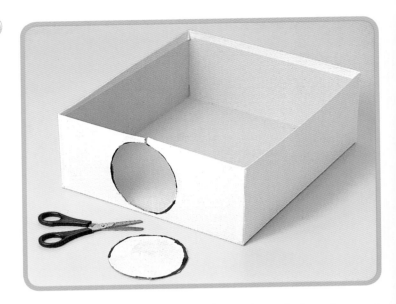

1. Trace around the circular object to draw a hole on one side of the box. The hole should be big enough for your hand to reach through. Cut out the hole by cutting down from the top.

2. Paint the outside of the box and lid. You may need several coats to cover them completely.

3

Cut the fabric in half and tape the top edges to the inside of the box. It should cover the hole like a pair of curtains.

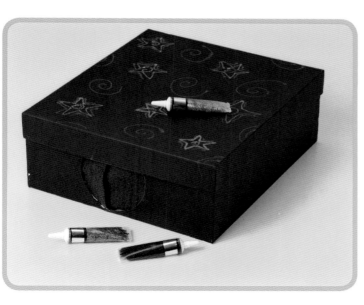

Decorate the box with glitter and colorful patterns. When it is dry, fill it with mystery items. Now you are ready to test your friends. Can they guess what is inside, just by feeling the items?

DID YOU KNOW?
Your fingertips are the most sensitive parts of your body.

Fill your box with things like sponges, pinecones, or plastic spiders. It's fun to guess fruit and vegetables, too.

STORY THEATER

YOU WILL NEED

- Shoe box
- Scissors
- Colored paper
- Colored pens and crayons
- Glitter glue
- Adhesive tape
- Thin cardboard
- Wooden skewers or craft sticks

1

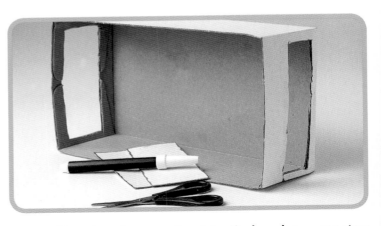

Stand the shoe box on its side. Cut out an opening at each end. Your "actors" will enter the stage from these openings, so make sure they are tall and wide enough.

2

Make curtains and frills for the front of the theater with colored paper. Use a black pen to mark the gathers. Use glitter glue for extra sparkle.

3

KIDS

Glue the curtains into place, using tape for the corners.

4

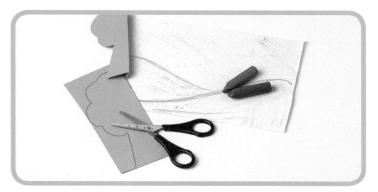

Cut a piece of paper the same size as the shoe box and draw a scene on it. Glue it to the inside of the box as the backdrop.

5

Cut out colored paper shapes to match your scenery and stick them to the inside edges of the curtains; these will be the wing flats.

6

Draw some characters on the shoe box lid. Color them in and cut them out. Make sure they fit through the side entrances to the stage. Use tape to attach them to the wooden skewers or craft sticks.

DID YOU KNOW?
A theater is a place people visit to see stories, called plays, acted out on a stage.

Make up your very own story to act out on your stage for your friends and family.

SCENTED CHARMS

YOU WILL NEED

- 2 cups flour
- 1 cup salt
- 1 cup water
- Large bowl
- Wooden spoon
- Rolling pin
- Shaped cookie cutters
- Baking sheet
- 1 drinking straw
- Acrylic paints and paintbrush
- Sweet-smelling essential oil (e.g. lavender)

1

To make the dough, place the flour, salt, and water in a large bowl. Stir the mixture until it forms a dough. Remove from the bowl and knead for five minutes.

2

KIDS

Roll out the dough on a lightly floured surface and cut out any shapes you like with the cookie cutters.

3

Place them on a greased baking sheet. Poke a hole in each shape with the end of a drinking straw. With a grown-up's help, bake the shapes in the oven at 265°F, for four hours. Let cool.

4

DS

Paint the shapes on both sides, leaving an area on the back unpainted. Drip a few drops of essential oil onto this patch, to give the charm its fragrance.

5

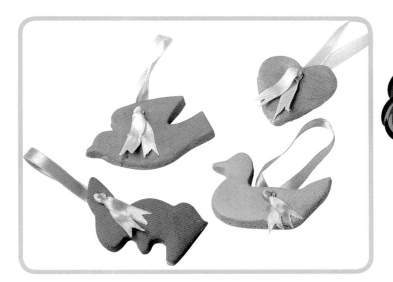

Push a length of ribbon through the hole. Tie a knot and hang the charm in the window or on the wall.

DID YOU KNOW?
Even doctors have sometimes used sweet-smelling oils to make people feel better.

FRIDGE MAGNETS

YOU WILL NEED

- Oven-bake clay in a variety of colors
- Modeling tool
- Baking sheet
- Aluminum foil
- Magnets
- Strong white glue

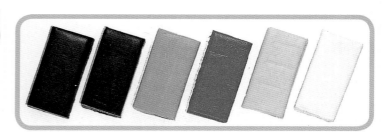

Knead the clay in your hand until it is soft enough to shape.

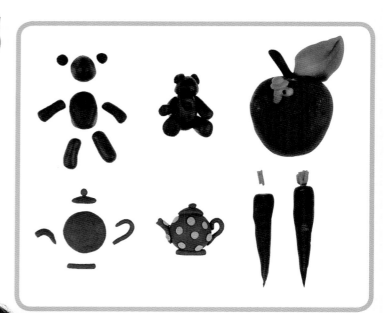

Experiment with the clay to make different items to decorate your fridge magnets. You could try making animals, faces, a teapot, fruits, or vegetables. You could even make a teddy bear from brown clay.

③

Press a magnet into the back of each clay item, then remove it before baking. Bake your objects in the oven, on a foil-covered baking sheet, following the manufacturer's instructions. Make sure you ask a grown-up for help. Once cool, glue the magnet in place.

Elmo is going to make the letters of his name: ELMO.

DID YOU KNOW?
Magnets stick to anything made of, or containing, a metal called iron.

DOUGH BASKETS

YOU WILL NEED

- Wooden spoon
- Large bowl
- 2 cups flour
- 1 cup salt
- 1 cup water
- Rolling pin
- Knife
- Shallow ovenproof dish
- Aluminum foil
- Acrylic paint and paintbrushes
- Water-based varnish

1

Use a wooden spoon to mix the flour, salt, and water together in a large bowl. When it forms a ball, take it out of the bowl and knead it for five minutes.

2

When the dough is smooth, roll it out thinly onto a floured surface and cut it into five strips about an inch wide.

Line a dish with foil. Weave the strips over and under each other, criss-crossing them to cover the bowl.

4

Press a long strip of dough around the rim of the basket to seal the edges. If you want, use leftover dough to make flowers or fruits to decorate it. Bake the basket for four hours at 275°F, or until it is completely dry.

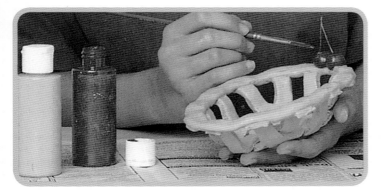

When the basket is cool, take it out of the bowl, then paint and varnish it.

DID YOU KNOW?
Salt dough is NOT for eating!

EGG CUP BUDDY

YOU WILL NEED

- Pack air-drying clay
- Modeling tool
- 1 egg
- Tray
- Acrylic paints and paintbrush
- Varnish and brush

1

Shape a block of clay to make Humpty's wall. Using an egg to gauge the size, use your thumbs to create the egg cup shape out of a ball of clay.

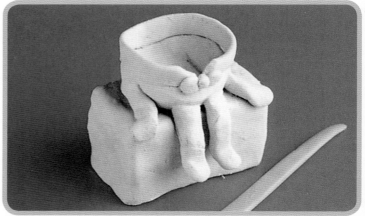

2

Make Humpty's arms and legs from sausage shapes. Attach the cup to the wall, using a little water to help it stick. Then attach Humpty's arms and legs in the same way. Make a clay necktie and press it in place. Leave to dry for 24 hours.

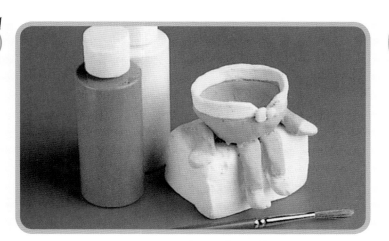

Paint your model one color at a time, allowing each to dry completely.

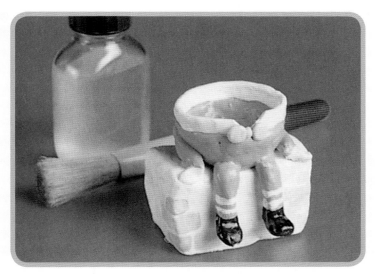

Leave for 2 hours and then varnish. Let dry.

DID YOU KNOW?
Most eggs have one yolk, though sometimes they have two. No-yolk eggs are called dwarf eggs.

TOAST RACK

YOU WILL NEED

- Cardboard box
- Scissors
- Strong white glue
- Water
- Old newspaper
- Acrylic paint
- Paintbrushes
- Water-based varnish

1

Cut out an oval base and four half-circles from a cardboard box.

2

Use the blade of the scissors to score the base, then tear out slots for the racks. Be careful not to cut all the way through. Remember to leave enough space for a slice of toast between the racks.

3

Glue the racks into place and leave to dry.

4
DS

Glue two layers of old newspaper all over the rack. Leave to dry between layers.

5
DS

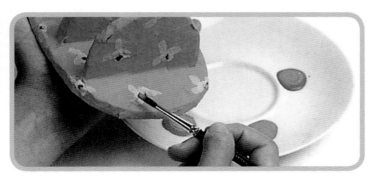

Paint and decorate your toast rack. When dry, add a coat of varnish and let dry.

DID YOU KNOW?
"French toast" is bread dipped in egg and milk, and cooked on a griddle.

TREAT TIME!

YOU WILL NEED

- 4 carrots, peeled
- 2 zucchini
- 4 stalks celery
- Half a cucumber
- 1 red bell pepper
- 1 yellow bell pepper
- 8 baby corns
- 1 cup low-fat cream cheese
- 2 tablespoons milk
- 2 scallions, finely chopped
- 1 tablespoon parsley
- 1 tablespoon chives
- Salt and pepper

1

Cut the carrots, zucchini, and celery into sticks two inches long. Halve the cucumber, remove the seeds, and cut into equal-sized sticks.

2

Halve the peppers and remove the seeds. Cut each into long strips.

Blue furry
monsters love
vegetables!

Make the cheesy dip by mixing the cream cheese and milk until smooth. Add the other ingredients, season with salt and pepper to taste, and stir until well mixed. Now it's ready to enjoy with your tasty, crunchy treats.

ICED COOKIES

YOU WILL NEED

- Wooden spoon
- Rolling pin
- Bowl
- Cookie cutters
- Baking sheet
- 1 ¾ cups plain flour
- 1 stick margarine or butter
- ⅓ cup sugar
- 1 teaspoon baking powder
- 1 egg
- Frosting, silver balls and sprinkles (optional)

- For plain cookies add:
  1 teaspoon vanilla extract
- For chocolate cookies add:
  3 tablespoons cocoa powder

Use a wooden spoon to mix the flour, margarine (or butter), vanilla extract (or cocoa powder), sugar, and baking powder, until it looks like breadcrumbs.

Add the egg and mix together until it forms a smooth dough.

Sprinkle a little flour onto the work surface and roll out the dough with a rolling pin. Do not press too hard. Use your cutters to cut out a selection of shapes.

4

Place the cookies on a greased baking tray. Bake for 15 minutes at 350°F.

Let cool and decorate with frosting, silver balls, and sprinkles.

DID YOU KNOW? In Great Britain, cookies are called "biscuits."

Homemade cookies make great gifts — if me don't eat them first!

FLOWER CROWN

YOU WILL NEED

- 10 pipe cleaners
- Tissue paper (different colors)
- Scissors
- White glue and brush
- Pencil
- Craft gems

1

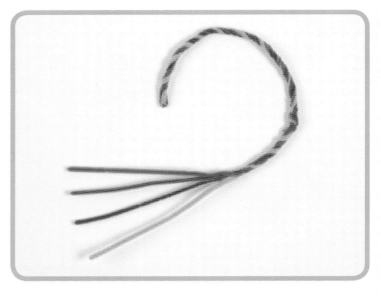

Twist four pipe cleaners together to make half the headband. Repeat this with four more, then twist the ends together to make the whole headband.

2

KIDS

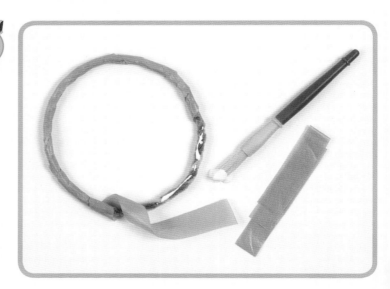

Brush glue over the headband. Wrap one inch-wide strips of green tissue paper around it, to cover it entirely.

③

Draw and cut out 42 tissue paper flower shapes. Snip the last two pipe cleaners into pieces 2 inches long. Layer six tissue flowers together then push a bent piece of pipe cleaner in then out of the middle, so both ends stick out.

④

Twist the ends of the pipe cleaners around the hoop to attach the flowers to the headband. Trim off the ends of the pipe cleaner. Carefully scrunch the petals, and glue craft gems in the middle of each flower.

PICNIC EMPANADAS

YOU WILL NEED

- Bowl
- Tablespoon
- Rolling pin
- Small plate
- Knife
- Baking sheet
- Fork
- Pastry brush

Pastry:
- 1½ cups plain flour
- ¾ cup margarine or butter
- 1 teaspoon water

Filling:
- 1 cup cooked, diced potato
- 1 medium onion, chopped
- 1 cup cheese, grated
- 1 egg, beaten
- Salt and pepper (to taste)

1

Place the flour and margarine (or butter) in a bowl, and use your fingers to mix it until it looks like breadcrumbs. Add a tablespoon of water and mix well, to make a ball.

2

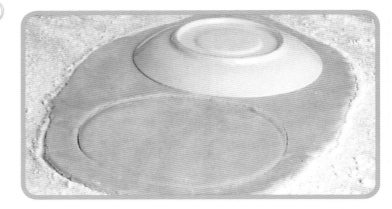

Roll out the pastry to a thickness of a quarter of an inch. Use a plate to mark out circles. Cut them out with a knife.

3

KIDS

Measure the filling ingredients and add them to a bowl. Mix them well, adding salt and pepper to taste.

Place the pastry circles on a greased baking sheet. Put a spoonful of filling in the middle of each. Brush a little beaten egg on the edges of the pastry.

5

Fold over the pastry to cover the filling. Use the fork to press down and seal the edges. Brush beaten egg over each finished empanada and bake for 25 minutes at 350°F, until golden brown.

DID YOU KNOW?
An empanada is a stuffed bread or pastry. It comes from Spain.

Use any bits of leftover pastry to make jam tarts.

ANYTIME CRAFTS

JEWELRY BOX

YOU WILL NEED

- Box with lid
- Scissors
- Old newspaper
- White glue
- Colored fabric or felt
- Gold paint, glitter, and sequins
- Shiny buttons or craft jewels

1

Cut the newspaper into squares and glue two layers all over the box and lid. Leave to dry between layers. You could also glue a piece of colored fabric or felt inside the box to line it.

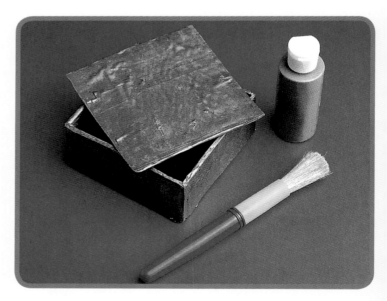

2

Paint the box and lid inside and out with gold paint. You may need two coats to cover them completely.

When the paint is dry, decorate the lid and sides of the box with glitter, paint, sequins, and recycled buttons or jewels.

DID YOU KNOW? Your gold jewelry is out of this world! Gold was floating around in space before our planet Earth was even formed!

Tie a pretty ribbon around your box to decorate the sides!

YOU WILL NEED

- Corrugated cardboard from a grocery box
- Ruler
- Pencil
- Scissors
- Adhesive tape
- Old newspaper
- White glue
- Acrylic paint
- Paintbrushes
- Tissue paper

Measure and cut out two squares the same size for the box base and lid. Then measure four small rectangles for the box sides. Their longest edge should be slightly shorter than the sides of the base.

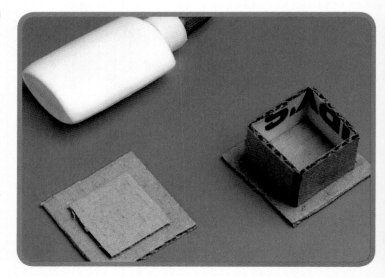

Use tape or glue to hold the box together. Use the top of the box to help you draw a small square to stick on the inside of the lid. Check that the lid fits into the box.

Glue two layers of newspaper squares over the box and lid. Check the lid still fits, then leave in a warm airy place to dry.

When the newspaper is dry, paint a base coat of color. You may need to paint a second coat to cover them completely. When dry, decorate the box and lid any way you wish.

DID YOU KNOW?
Real gemstones are found underground. They are dug up, then cut and polished to make them shine.

Scrunch up tissue paper and put it inside your box, before you put trinkets in it.

YOU WILL NEED

- Felt squares: various colors
- Scissors
- Fabric glue
- Rubber band
- Needle and colored embroidery thread
- Polyester stuffing
- Ribbon

1

Cut three squares of colored felt, each slightly smaller than the last. Layer them, using a little glue to hold them in place.

2

Now roll the felt up tightly into a sausage, using glue to stick it. You will need to hold the sausage in place with a rubber band while the glue dries.

3

KIDS

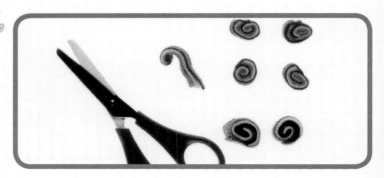

When the glue is thoroughly dry, use scissors to cut the sausage into beads.

④

To make a heart pendant, use two squares of colored felt. Cut out a heart from each color, making one smaller than the other.

⑤

Place a little stuffing between the layers and sew them together with colored thread. Make a ribbon loop at the top for threading.

⑥

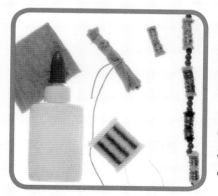

To make these beads, roll a small square of felt. Hold in place with glue, then wind colored thread around it to make decorative bands.

YOU WILL NEED

- Clean, old glasses, jars, and bottles
- Black outliner
- Paintbrush
- Water-soluble glass paints

1

Before you begin, wash and dry the glass. Use the black outliner to draw a picture on the glass. Be sure there are no gaps for the glass paint to leak through.

 2

KIDS

When the black outline is completely dry use the paints to fill in the color. Wash the brush well between colors, and dry it before dipping it into the next color. Let dry.

DID YOU KNOW? People throw away a lot of glass jars and bottles. Try recycling them instead!

Thank-you, Elmo. I'll put it in a pretty vase.

211

FOIL FRAMES

YOU WILL NEED

- Thick cardboard
- Ruler
- Strong scissors
- Aluminum foil
- Gluestick
- Pencil and ballpoint pen

Cut out two cardboard squares, one with a square picture hole in the middle. Cut a foil square an inch larger than the frame.

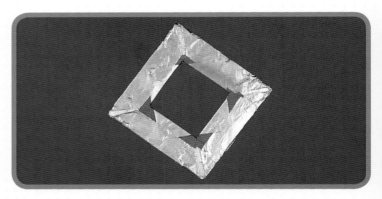

Spread the cardboard frame with glue. With clean fingers, gently press the foil over the frame. Tuck in the edges carefully, and smooth down the foil.

KIDS

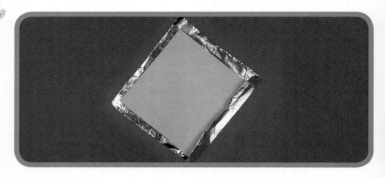

Cover the remaining square with foil. This is the back of the frame.

4

Attach the frame to the back with glue on three sides, leaving an opening at the top to slip in the photo.

5

KIDS

Use the ballpoint pen to mark a design onto the front of the frame. Don't press too hard or you might tear the foil.

You can make your frame any shape you like — a square, a rectangle, a circle, even a star!

MIRROR PAINTING

YOU WILL NEED

- Mirror tiles or small mirrors
- Black outliner
- Paintbrushes
- Water-soluble glass paints
- Paper towels (optional)

1

Use the outliner to draw a border on the mirror. Use it like a pen, squeezing gently to allow a steady stream of the paint onto the glass. Keep paper towels handy in case of spills.

2

KIDS

When the outliner is completely dry, you can paint in the color. Use a dry brush to dip into one color at a time. Wash and dry the brush well between colors.

FABRIC PRINTING

YOU WILL NEED

- Carrot, medium potato, apple
- Knife
- Kitchen towel
- Sponge
- Fabric paint: various colors
- Plain fabric
- Cookie cutters

1

Cut a carrot in half, longways. Use the sponge to spread a little fabric paint onto the flat side of the carrot.

2
KIDS

Gently press the carrot down onto the fabric. Do not move it about, or the paint will smudge. Print a row of carrots. Leave the printed fabric in a safe place to dry. Follow the directions that come with the fabric paint to set the dye.

3

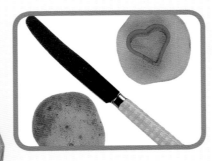

Cut a potato in half. Press the cookie cutter firmly into the potato and cut away the potato around the outside. Remove the cutter, and pat the stamp dry with a kitchen towel, so it's ready for printing.

4
DS

Use a sponge to apply fabric paint to the stamp. Print your pattern.

5

Cut an apple in half and pat it dry with a kitchen towel.

6
DS

Use the sponge to apply fabric paint to the apple surface and press it down firmly onto the fabric.

DID YOU KNOW?
Carrots grow underground. They are called root vegetables, because the part we eat is actually a root.

Cut up the fabric into rectangles and print on them, to make place mats or napkins for all your family.

NOTEPAPER

YOU WILL NEED

- Paper: blue, white, green
- Black marker
- Scissors
- White glue
- Hole punch

1 Decorate the blue sheet of paper first. Draw, then cut out, small fluffy white clouds and glue them onto the sky.

2 Decide how low the skyline will be, then draw and cut a wavy line across the top of a sheet of green paper to make hills. Glue the green paper on top of the blue to create a scene.

3

4

KIDS

Make a snow scene decorated with a cheerful snowman. Draw a snowman on a white sheet of paper. Remember to draw the horizon, too. Use scissors to cut out the snowman and horizon, then glue the sheet of white paper onto the blue sky.

Decorate the snowman using a black marker to make his face. Use a hole punch to make lots of tiny white circles for snowflakes, then stick them on your snowy scene.

ENVELOPES

YOU WILL NEED

- Occasion card: birthday, holidays, Valentine
- Colored paper
- Scissors
- Glue
- Colored markers

1 KIDS

Place your card in the center of the paper. Fold up the bottom of the sheet to cover the card completely. Leave an inch at the top, and ½ inch on each side.

2 KIDS

Fold the top flap down, over the card.

Open out the paper completely and fold in the sides over the card. Make sure the card fits easily the folded shape.

Trim the excess paper from the sides of the front flap using the folds to guide you. This will make it easier to close your envelope.

(5)

Cut in at angles on either side of the top flap to shape it.

(6)

IDS

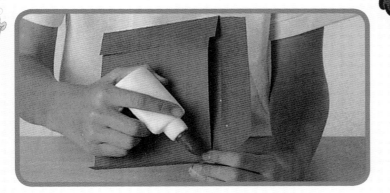

Use glue to hold the envelope's shape.

DID YOU KNOW?
Zip codes are numbers after your address that help the Post Office deliver mail to the right house or building.

Elmo likes to decorate the envelope with markers or crayons.

YOU WILL NEED

- Plain ribbon
- Colored markers
- Ruler
- Scissors
- Needle and thread (to match ribbon)

1
KIDS

Use colored markers to decorate plain ribbon. Cut a little ribbon off to practice on first. Don't press too hard or the color will bleed across the weave of the ribbon and spoil it. Use one color at a time before moving on to the next. Repeating your pattern will give the ribbon a nice look.

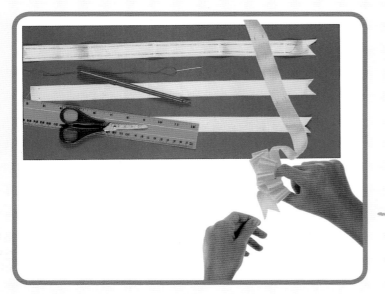

Spread a 24-inch length of ribbon across the work surface. Use a marker and ruler to make a tiny mark every 2 inches. Thread the needle with thread about 8 inches longer than the ribbon and make a knot at the end. Sew a small stitch at each mark on the ribbon. Now pull gently at the thread and the ribbon should bunch up, making a fancy bow.

POP-UP CARDS

YOU WILL NEED

- Colored thin cardboard
- Scissors
- Ruler
- White glue
- Colored paper
- Colored markers

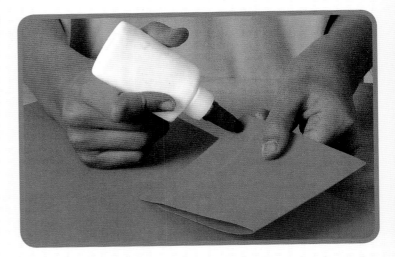

Fold a sheet of cardboard in half, then open it out. Now cut a smaller rectangle and fold in half. Fold a lip along the two shorter edges and glue them to the inside of the larger card to make the vase. Check the vase flattens when the card is shut.

Cut stems and leaves out of green paper, and glue them inside the vase. Cut out some paper flowers and glue them onto the stems, making sure they are hidden when the card is closed.

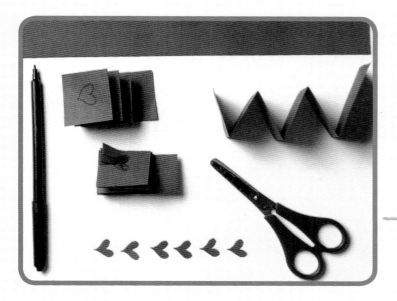

Cut lots of small hearts from folded red paper to decorate the vase.

Decorate the front of the card with a large paper heart, then glue a smaller one in a contrasting color in the middle. Now you are ready to write your message inside the card.

DID YOU KNOW? The heart that beats inside your body doesn't look at all like the heart shapes you see on Valentine's Day!

YOU WILL NEED

- Thin cardboard
- Colored paper
- Ruler
- Colored markers
- Scissors
- Glue

1

Fold a sheet of thin cardboard in half to make the card. Use a ruler to mark two dots on either side of the central fold. They should be evenly spaced. These are where the concertina ends will be fixed.

2

Draw a clown with the arms ending at the dots. Try to keep the picture simple.

3

KIDS

Color in your picture, making it bright and colorful.

Cut a long thin strip of paper to make the concertina. Fold it one way, then the other, to form a fan. Press the folds down firmly with your thumb.

5

Glue each end of the concertina to the end of the clown's arms. Open and close the card a few times to make sure the concertina opens and closes easily.

DID YOU KNOW?
Long ago, clowns were called "fools" or "jesters."

Don't forget to decorate the front of your card, too!

YOU WILL NEED

- Thin cardboard or paper: white
- Scissors
- Colored markers
- Clear plastic folder
- Adhesive tape

①

Take a sheet of thin cardboard or paper and fold it into three equal sections as shown in the picture.

②

On the front flap mark out a rectangle and the finger grip space. Cut away the finger grip space.

③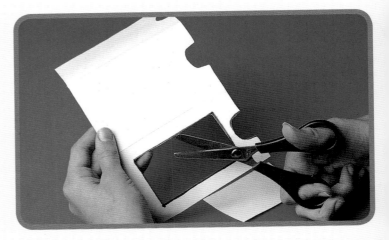

Open out the cardboard and cut out the rectangle. This is the front frame of the card.

4
KIDS

Decorate the front frame with a pattern. Cut a piece of paper the same size as one section of the card and draw on your design.

5

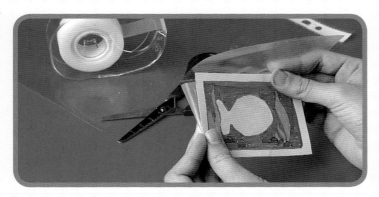

Slip your picture into the plastic folder with the top against a fold. Trim the plastic to fit the picture. Tape the back to the plastic.

6

Use a black marker to draw an outline of the picture on the plastic.

7
KIDS

Open out the card, and slip the bottom flap between your picture and the plastic layer on top. The bottom flap is now between the two. Fold the frame down over the top. Grip the plastic and paper and pull; the picture will magically appear in color as you pull it out.

TRASH CAN

YOU WILL NEED

- Old dinner plate
- Pencil
- Thick cardboard
- Scissors
- Large rubber band
- White glue
- Masking tape
- Gift wrap
- Colored paper

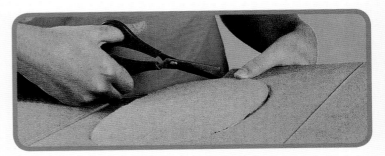

Draw around a dinner plate onto thick cardboard and cut out to make the base of the trash can.

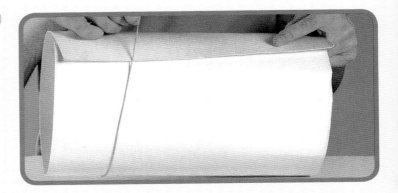

Cut out the wall of the can from thick cardboard. Check it fits around the base and overlaps by 2 inches. Hold in place with the rubber band.

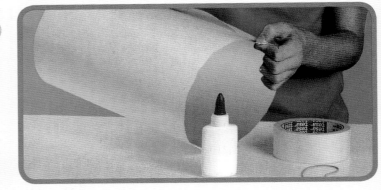

Stick a length of masking tape along one of the wall's long edges, but don't stick it down yet.

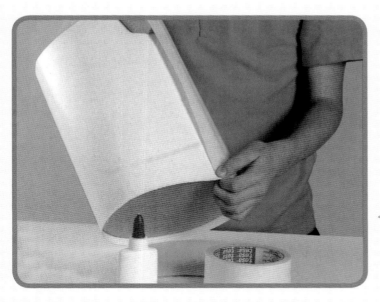

Decorate your trash can with a theme—dinosaurs, animals, space— whatever you like! Now scram!

Put glue around the outside edge of the base. Fit the wall around the base, then press down the masking tape to hold it all together.

5

'DS

Your trash can is now ready to decorate with colorful wrapping paper or cut-out paper shapes.

YOU WILL NEED

- Thick cardboard
- Scissors
- Quilt batting
- Patterned fabric
- Fabric glue
- Plain fabric
- Rubber band
- Strong glue

1

Cut out a rectangle of thick cardboard for the base. Use this to measure out the four sides. Cut out a lid the same size as the base. These pieces will be the "outer box." Now cut out an identical set of pieces. Trim ¼ inch off all around the edges of the second set to make the "inner box."

2

KIDS

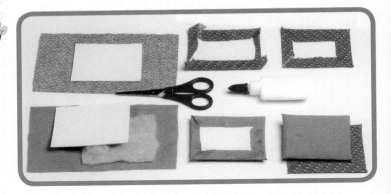

Glue a piece of quilt batting to the four sides of the outer box and cover each one with patterned fabric. Cover the "outer" lid and base with patterned fabric. Glue a piece of batting to each piece of the "inner" box, including the lid and base, then cover these with plain fabric.

3

Glue the "inner" pieces to the matching "outer" pieces. Then use the strong glue to stick the whole box together and hold it in place with the rubber band while it dries.

4

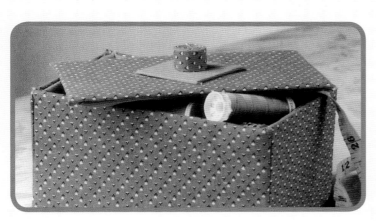

To decorate the lid, cover a small square piece of cardboard with plain fabric. Glue this onto the lid. Now cut a strip of fabric, cover one side with glue and roll it up lengthwise. Glue onto the lid as a handle.

DID YOU KNOW?
Decorating fabric with neat stitches of colored thread is called embroidery.

You can also use it to hold handkerchiefs, hairbands, and scrunchies.

ORIGAMI BOX

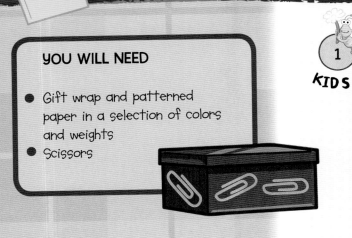

1 KIDS

Fold a rectangle of paper in half lengthwise.

2 KIDS

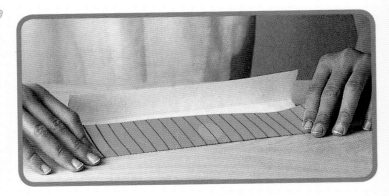

Fold each half into the middle so you have 4 equal sections.

3

Make a narrow fold outward from both long edges.

4

Fold in the corners and tuck them under the small fold.

5

6

Place your fingers in the corners and carefully open out the box into shape. Use your fingers to make folds at the four corners.

DID YOU KNOW? To make a real origami model, you don't need scissors or glue—just paper to fold.

YOU WILL NEED

- Colored paper
- Colored tissue paper
- Scissors
- White glue

1

KIDS

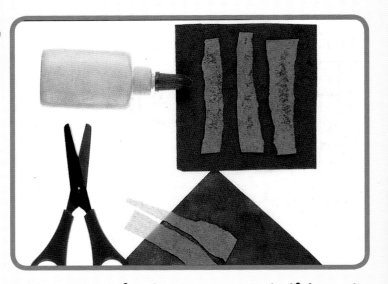

Fold a piece of colored paper in half to make the card. Tear off pieces of colored tissue paper and glue them onto the card.

2

KIDS

Layer on strips of different colored tissue paper, or make a picture using different colors and shapes. When the glue is dry, your card is ready for you to write a special message inside.

③

To make an eye-catching Valentine card, layer four pieces of red tissue paper together, fold them in half, and tear out a heart shape. Stick the hearts on top of each other in the middle of the card. The border of the card is made from strips of red tissue paper.

MAIL

YOU WILL NEED

- Extra long colored pipe cleaners
- Marker pen
- Corks

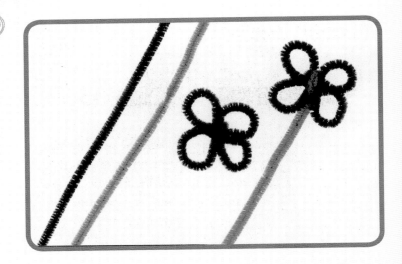

①

Bend a colorful pipe cleaner into a flower shape. Then twist a long green pipe cleaner around the center of the flower to make a stalk.

② KIDS

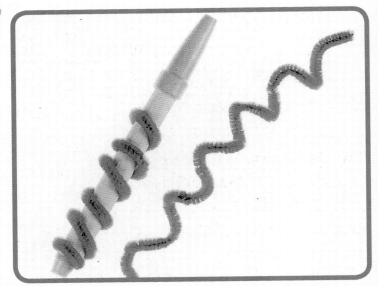

Make "leaves" by winding green pipe cleaners around a pen to make spiral shapes. Ease the spirals off the pen. Put the flowers and leaves into a vase.

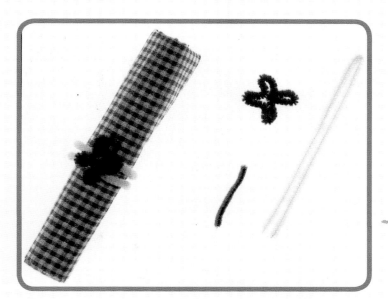

To make a napkin holder, bend a pipe cleaner in half, then into a circle. Decorate it with a flower, fixed in place with a short piece of pipe cleaner.

4

Shape sparkly pipe cleaners into attractive table decorations. Push the shaped wire into cork to make a stand.

DID YOU KNOW?
Be careful! The ends of pipe cleaners can be sharp!

If you make a mistake, straighten out the pipe cleaner, and POOF! You can begin again!

YOU WILL NEED

- Picture you have drawn or one from a magazine
- Thin cardboard (same size as your picture)
- White glue
- Ruler
- Pencil
- Scissors

1 KIDS

Glue your picture onto a piece of thin cardboard, making sure every part of the picture—even the edges—is firmly glued down.

2

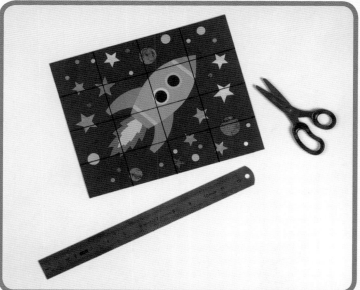

Divide the picture into evenly sized pieces with a pencil and ruler. Carefully cut the picture into pieces along the pencil lines.

DID YOU KNOW?
The biggest jigsaw in the world is bigger than a ping-pong table and has over 18,000 pieces!

Jumble up the pieces, then try to complete your picture puzzle.

I bet you are a SUPER puzzle-doer!

Keep all the puzzle pieces in an envelope so they don't get lost.

YOU WILL NEED

- Sheet white paper
- Ruler
- Pencil
- Colored paper
- Scissors
- White glue
- Clear contact paper

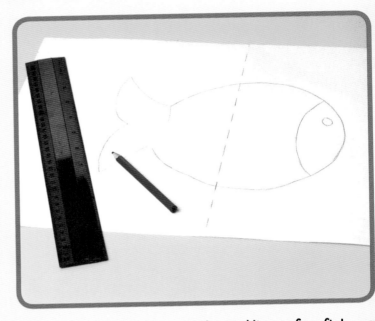

Begin by drawing a simple outline of a fish, or anything else, on your paper. Make sure that the picture is in the middle.

Decide which colors you want for your picture, then use a ruler and pencil to measure out lots of small squares on colored paper. Cut them out. Make sure you have plenty of each color.

DID YOU KNOW?
The ancient Romans, used tiny mosaic tiles to make wonderful pictures on floors and walls.

Elmo made place mats for Elmo's whole family to use at dinnertime!

Glue the squares onto your picture. Begin in the top corner, and work from one side to the other.

4

Your finished mosaic should look something like this. To protect it, ask a grown-up to cover it with a layer of clear contact paper.

YOU WILL NEED

- Colored paper and envelopes
- Selection of self-adhesive stickers

1

KIDS

Decorate sheets of brightly colored paper with the stickers. These rainbow stickers look great centered at the top of the page.

2

KIDS

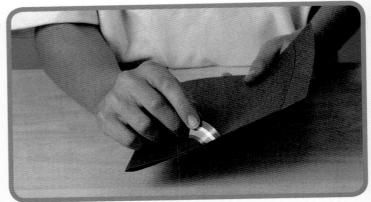

Make matching envelopes for your writing paper by placing a matching sticker on the bottom left-hand corner. Use the same color paper for the envelope, or another color that matches.

To make a folder for your decorated paper and envelopes, fold up a large sheet of paper, three quarters of its length, leaving a piece to fold down into a flap.

Hold the sides of the folder together with more stickers, then decorate the front with matching stickers.

DID YOU KNOW?
A rainbow is always made up of seven colors—red, orange, yellow, green, blue, indigo, and violet.

I'm going to write a letter to my best friend, Big Bird.

SILHOUETTE CARDS

YOU WILL NEED

- Black paper
- Colored paper
- Wax or pencil crayon
- Scissors
- Glue

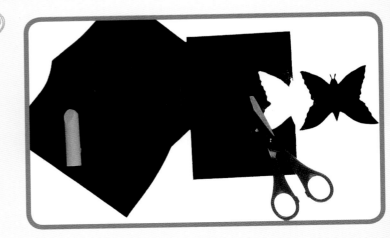

1

Fold a sheet of black paper in half. Draw half a butterfly, or other object, on one side of the folded paper, and cut it out.

2

KIDS

Make a card from a folded sheet of colored paper. Glue a piece of white paper onto the front of the card. Glue the butterfly silhouette onto the piece of white paper to finish the card.

DID YOU KNOW?
A silhouette
is the outline of an
object, filled in with
solid color.

For a Halloween card, fold a sheet of orange or yellow paper in half and glue on a black background, leaving a border around the edge. Fold another piece of orange or yellow paper in half, draw on half a pumpkin head.

4
DS

Cut out the pumpkin head and glue it onto the black background on the front of the card.

CLAY JEWELRY

YOU WILL NEED

- Oven-bake clay in a variety of colors
- Modeling tool
- Baking sheet
- Varnish
- Pin backs
- Strong glue

1 KIDS

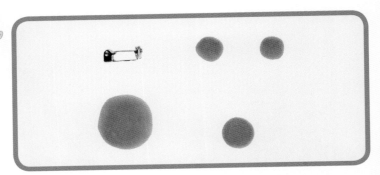

To make a pig pin, start with a disk of pink clay for the face, a small disk for the snout, and two small balls for the ears.

2

Shape the two balls into teardrop shapes for ears. Mark nostrils on the snout with the modeling tool. Make two eyes from black clay.

3

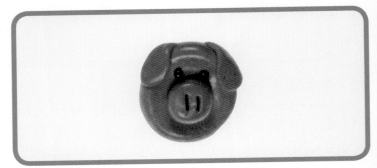

Stick the snout, ears, and eyes to the face using a little water. Put on a baking sheet and follow the manufacturer's instructions.

4

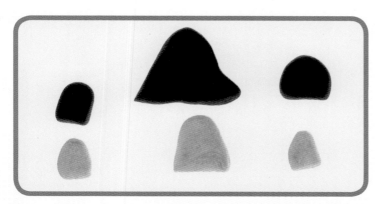

To make a toadstool pin, make three yellow
stalks, one large and two small. Now make the
red caps and press them carefully onto the
stalks. Gently squish the toadstools together
into a clump.

5

IDS

Decorate the toadstools with tiny yellow
dots. Your pin is now ready for baking.

6

When cool, varnish your jewelry. Allow to dry,
then glue on the pin backs with the help of a
grown-up.

STAINED GLASS

YOU WILL NEED

- Paper: black, white
- Black marker
- Scissors
- Clear blue cellophane
- Glue
- Glitter glue

①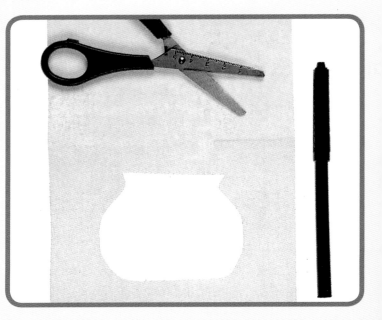

Fold a sheet of paper in half and draw a fish-bowl shape on the front. Cut out carefully, making sure not to cut outside the bowl's outline.

②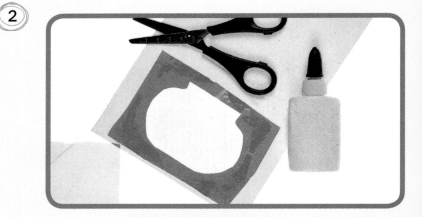

Cut a rectangle of clear blue cellophane to cover the fish bowl shape. Glue it inside the card. Let dry.

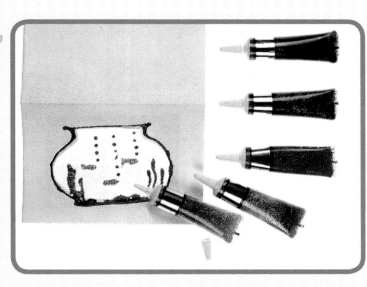

Use glitter glue to decorate the bowl with fish, seaweed, and pebbles. Decorate the edge of the bowl as well.

4

Have fun experimenting with lots of different designs. Simple shapes work the best.

DID YOU KNOW?
Stained glass windows are made of colored glass panes, held together by lead, zinc, or copper.

Elmo likes to put the cards on a windowsill so the light shines through them!

YOU WILL NEED

- Colored construction paper
- Pencil
- Scissors
- Thick cardboard
- Crayons or paint
- White glue

①

Draw four tulip flowers on colored paper and cut them out. Copy two leaf-shaped sides and two base shapes on thick cardboard as shown, and cut them out. The bottom edges need to be straight to help them stand. Now color them in.

②

Slot the letter rack together. You may need to make a rough one first to get the shape and slots right.

Glue two tulip flowers back-to-back on each stem.

4

Leave the letter rack to dry. It is now ready to hold your mail.

YOU WILL NEED

- Cardboard tubes
- Ruler and pencil
- Scissors
- Cork
- Acrylic paints
- Paintbrush
- Old saucer
- Thin cardboard
- Glue
- Two googly eyes
- Red paper for tongue
- Ribbon 1 x 6 inches long
- Adhesive tape

1

Cut the cardboard tubes into one inch sections. You will need about 10 altogether. Paint them green. Paint the cork green.

2

KIDS

Add paint colors to the old saucer and use your fingertips to make patterns on the green tube sections. Leave to dry.

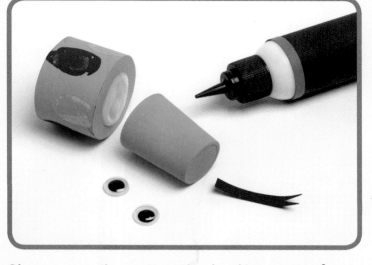

Glue a cardboard circle to the end of one section, then glue on the cork for the head. Add the eyes and a tongue. Leave to dry.

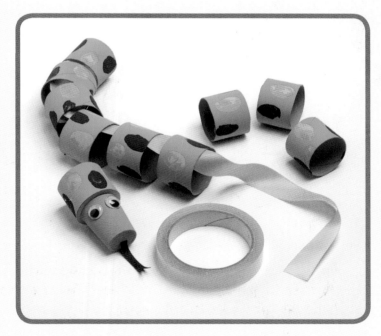

To join the snake together, thread the ribbon through the tube sections. Tape the ribbon to the inside of each tube, one at a time.

DID YOU KNOW?
The anaconda is the biggest snake in the world. It can be as big around its middle as a full-grown man!

Hisss! Elmo can hiss like a wriggly snake. Can you?

INDEX

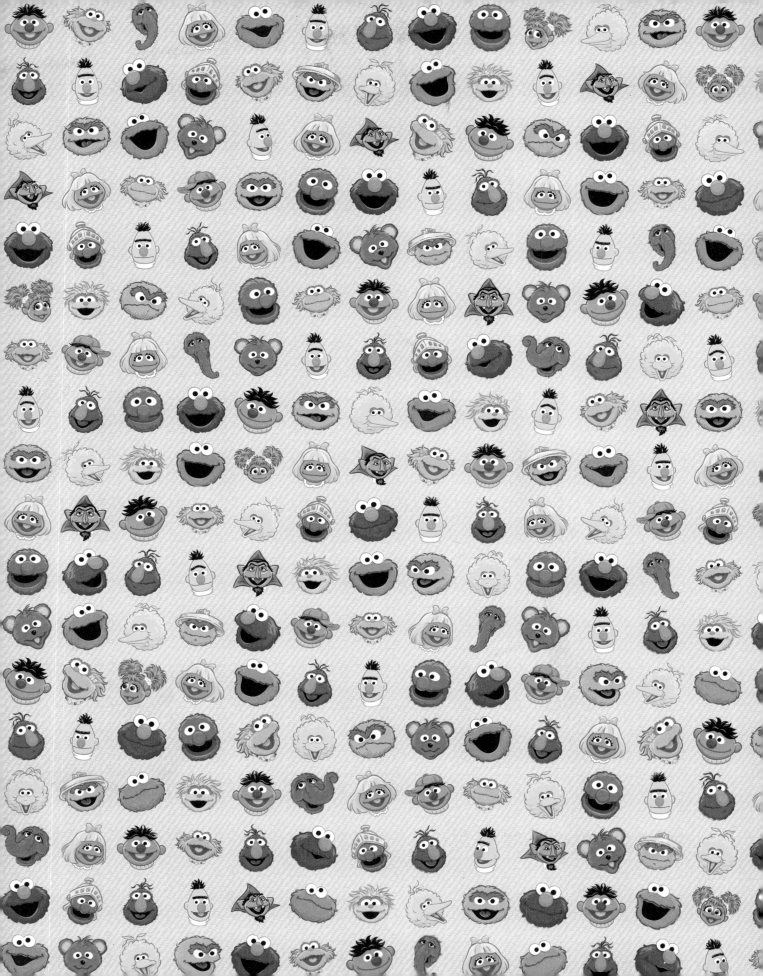